D1009391

PRAISE FOR

Defending Ourselves

Defending Ourselves makes an important contribution to the literature on sexual violence against women; it tells us women's own stories of rape and survival—in their own words; it teaches us the power and limitations of self defense; and it offers women hope and guidance as they face the long journey to recovery.
> —Leslie R. Wolfe, Ph.D.
> President, Center for Women Policy Studies

Wiseman does an excellent job of addressing a difficult subject. This book is chock-full of valuable information.
> —Donna S. Chaiet
> President, Prepare, New York

A must read for women of all ages. Mothers should make it required reading for their daughters.

One of the great accomplishments of *Defending Ourselves* is that it is thought-provoking without making every woman a victim and every man a potential rapist.
> —Phyllis Greenberger, MSW
> Executive Director, Society for the Advancement of
> Women's Health

Wiseman finally charges women with taking control of their sexual destiny. Her comprehensive approach to understanding the complexities of stranger and date rape is just in time.
> —Phillip R. Stirling, Deputy District Attorney
> Los Angeles County

Defending Ourselves

A GUIDE TO PREVENTION, SELF-DEFENSE, AND RECOVERY FROM RAPE

Rosalind Wiseman

ILLUSTRATIONS BY JAMES EDWARDS

THE NOONDAY PRESS / *Farrar, Straus and Giroux, New York*

LIBRARY OF CONGRESS CATALOGING-IN-PUBLICATION DATA
Wiseman, Rosalind
Defending ourselves : a guide to prevention, self-defense, and
recovery from rape / Rosalind Wiseman.—1st ed.
p.   cm.
1. Rape—Prevention. 2. Self-defense for women.   I. Title.
HV6558.W57   1995   362.88′3—dc20   94–12468   CIP

Excerpt from "I Be Your Water" by Bernice Johnson Reagon/Sweet
Honey in the Rock, reprinted by permission of Bernice Johnson Reagon,
Songtalk Publishing.

ACKNOWLEDGMENTS

How to even begin thanking the individuals who have helped me make this book a reality is difficult. I have been blessed by the support of a large group of people.

To my dear friends Trina and Ted, who gave me the unconditional love and support to leave an abusive relationship and who continue to provide insight, perspective, and laughter in my life. To Sharon and Jackie, whose initial suggestions changed the direction of the book and my thinking. To my Block Island family, for their invaluable discussions of the book. To Melissa Buckley, for researching and writing the skeleton for chapter 5 (it is a great chapter because of you) and for all the other advice about the book. To Emily Irish, for being the hippest intern and researching and organizing the sexual-assault-center directory. To Catie Lazarus, for having the courage to trust me and tell her story. To Enid Maren and Catherine Fleischer, for editing and researching.

Thanks to Eagle Rock Karate and all my friends there, who have alternated between beating me up and patting me on the back. I will always have a lot to learn from you.

To Elisabeth Kallick Dyssegaard, at Farrar, Straus and Giroux, for being the coolest, most persistent editor and for occasionally letting me have my own way. To Chris Tomasino and Jonathan, for being in my corner and steering me the right way.

To my father, for loving to talk about what I do and for giving me the opportunity to write the book in the first place. To Leslie Wolfe, for thinking of me when asked if she knew anyone interested in writing a book on this topic.

To Jeff and Nancy, for coming up with the title. Maybe next time . . .

To my family (including my aunts, the big three), because this has been a very difficult year and, somehow, we are surviving.

Lastly, my thanks to James, for everything. Besides your technical expertise, your love, loyalty, gentleness, and honesty have helped me complete this book. I am lucky to have you in my life.

CONTENTS

*If there is no struggle, there is no progress. Power concedes nothing
without a demand.*   FREDERICK DOUGLASS

> *As I gave power to the sound of my own voice*
> *A way broke before me, I followed my choice*
> *I walked along the way other lives had been*
> *Till I came to what seemed like an end*
> *Again these hands, reaching, beckoning for me*
> *They knew exactly who and what I should be*

BERNICE JOHNSON REAGON/Sweet Honey in the Rock,
"I Be Your Water"

Defending
Ourselves

PREFACE

Three years ago I started Woman's Way, a company to train women in self-defense. I had recently graduated from college. I had also just received my first-degree black belt in karate and was keenly aware of how much that process increased my self-confidence. So when I was asked to teach a women's self-defense course at a high school, I jumped at the chance. As soon as I began teaching, I knew it was what I wanted to do. Today, Woman's Way and our nonprofit organization, the Empower Program, have expanded to provide training and education for people of all ages. We work within schools, universities, corporations, and sexual-assault centers, and facilitate gender-communication seminars on such issues as sexual harassment and date rape.

I do this work for a lot of reasons. One of them is that as a teenager I was involved in an abusive relationship. It was the most emotionally painful experience I have had. I was never raped, but my response to the abuse was similar to that of rape survivors. For this reason, I feel that I am better able to understand what they are going through and can steer them away from thinking of themselves as victims. I think it is important for women to tell their stories, while it is equally important that women who have survived an assault from a stranger or a "loved one" are not solely perceived as products of the victimization they have experienced.

I have included my experience because for years I believed that there would never be a time when the experience was not a part of my daily thoughts. I also doubted I could reach the point where I would be able to have a safe, healthy relationship with a man. Now I can. I have learned that people do survive terrible, traumatic experiences. If I can, every woman can.

There was no obvious reason why I would be vulnerable to this kind of experience. I had a loving, supportive family. I had no need to rebel against my parents, because they always respected me and the decisions I made. We had our fights but we communicated well, and even when my parents disagreed with something I did, I knew they would let me make mistakes and still love me. I went to a wonderful school where I was close to many of the teachers and received an excellent education. I was a competitive tennis player.

But like so many girls, by the time I entered high school I felt ugly, unpopular, and insecure. I was fourteen and I fell in love with Michael, the "pretty boy" of the class. He seemed confident and had everything going for him. He was handsome, very wealthy, and incredibly charming. From the beginning I felt unworthy of his love, but for the next two years we were inseparable. Once I had this relationship, I felt tremendous pressure to maintain it because I believed my social status depended on it. Very quickly I began to think that I would be nothing without him.

The relationship turned abusive during my sophomore year, when he began to take his anger toward his family out on me. Naturally, Michael needed unconditional support and love from someone, and I felt special to be able to provide that for him. There were many nights when he would cry with his head in my lap because he felt he had failed in his family's eyes.

So why did I allow him to abuse me? I had the bad luck of becoming involved with a person in despair, and I had not been taught to establish boundaries between myself and others, especially those I loved. By the time I had been with him for two years, my identity was completely tied to his. I could make decisions only on the basis of how they would affect the two of us. As a result, I was caught in an increasingly confusing relationship without the tools to recognize how dangerous it was rapidly becoming.

One day we were standing at our lockers, having an argument, and Michael hit me in the face. I got a very bad bloody nose. Looking back, I realize that his hurting me was not out of the ordinary. I can vividly recall that I was glad, because he had finally injured me in a way that showed. From then on, things got steadily worse. He constantly told me I was stupid and he belittled everything I did. I once got so angry at him for this that I slapped him across the face. His response was to throw me up against a wall, put one hand around my throat and the other hand in front of my face, and say, "If you touch me again, I will kill you." I really believed he would. He had destroyed all the self-confidence I had. It never occurred to me to confide in anyone or to ask for help. I didn't really want anybody to know the truth, including myself. The worse it became, the more I wanted everyone to know that I had a perfect boyfriend and a perfect life—to compensate for the horror of the truth.

During the next two years I tried to break up with him several times, and each time he persuaded me to come back to him. By junior year, he started to drink and do a lot of drugs. Things got progressively worse. But, ironically, I had this defense mechanism that made me feel invincible. I needed to feel this way because if I admitted any weakness I would have to realize the extent of my problems.

By my junior year, Michael had begun to use sex to manipulate me. He soon had complete dominance in our sexual relationship. Usually he would put me in his mother's bed and blindfold me. I wasn't allowed to do or say anything. If I spoke, he would tell me to be quiet. Sometimes he would leave the room and listen through the door to make sure I was completely still. Every time sexual abuse occurred, he would say, "I love you. Why are you angry with me? I love you." I didn't realize that love does not justify or excuse abuse. I made myself believe that his love for me and the abuse were two separate entities, and that if I became "perfect"—doing everything he wanted—he would stop the abuse.

My senior year I became increasingly introverted and depressed. I couldn't eat, and before going to bed I would take NyQuil to help me sleep. His drug and alcohol use dramatically increased. I couldn't break up with him, because I didn't understand why he would treat me badly if he loved me. For most of the time I wasn't with him, I endlessly thought about why things were so wrong. He was cold to me at best, and physically and sexually abusive to me at worst. I desperately wanted him to be the person I had fallen in love with. But the more I tried, the angrier he became. As I couldn't distinguish my identity from his, he couldn't separate his self-loathing from his contempt for me. He hated and resented me for loving him.

I became withdrawn from my family, and my parents had no idea what to do. They had faith in me as a person, but they didn't know how to handle me because I looked so miserable.

I went to Occidental College in Los Angeles, California—at the other end of the country. My involvement with Michael did not stop; he called me anytime he felt suicidal. But he was not physically present to control me. I was also free from the lie I had maintained for years about our relationship. In Los Angeles, no one knew me and no one knew him. Even though I had come from a big city, the community was very small and close-knit. It was important to me that I could be in a place where I wouldn't be judged for who I had been in Washington, D.C.

I had to slowly relearn how to trust men, because by the time I got to college I could not be physically close to a man without flinching and lowering my head. Eventually I was able to tell a friend at school, Ted, about my experience. He was supportive, held my hand, and listened. But it took me months to talk about the abuse. Everything would be in my head, but I couldn't say the words out loud. Michael had conditioned me to tell no one, and I was used to making sure everything looked fine. I was also ashamed; I felt weak and out of control. Sometimes I felt so fragile that I believed I would shatter into millions of pieces.

During my sophomore year in college I stopped playing competitive tennis. But I had always been an athlete, so I wanted to do something. A friend invited me to see his karate test. I thought karate was beautiful and was immediately attracted to it. But learning martial arts wasn't easy. There were few women students in my school and it was a hard style, so we sparred a great deal. At first I closed my eyes when I fought, and I was terrified of hitting anyone. I had to yell—to get in touch with my physical and mental powers. When I first started, I had no confidence. But as I learned and grew accustomed to fighting with men, I felt my body gain strength. About a year after I began studying karate, all my anger about my relationship came out and I became very confrontational and violent toward men, wanting to beat them all up. I would visualize hitting or humiliating Michael, as he had done to me.

At first the martial arts brought out all my violence, but one day I had an experience that opened my eyes. During sparring class I was paired up with a young man about my age. Off the mat, a group of his friends were teasing him about fighting with a woman. I was enraged and fought as hard as I could. Within a few minutes, he was spitting up saliva, on his knees in pain. As I watched him, I realized how much I had hurt him, and I was not proud of what I had done. I caused him pain and humiliation. In that one moment I learned that winning the fight when you are the perpetrator is a degrading experience. Fighting with that guy was the beginning of my quest to understand the violence inside me. I needed to admit, understand, and accept this part of me. I knew I couldn't deny my anger, but I also needed to control it.

When I came home for the summer, I told Michael what I had learned over the last year, and, although I was terrified, I also told him that he had no right to do the things he had done to me. It was the first time in years that I was able to clearly distinguish myself from him. I had found my way and I was in control of my life. I needed to heal my body and my mind. Karate forced me to deal with the way I felt about my body and seriously challenged the limited perceptions I had had of my physical, mental, and emotional strength.

No one should go through what I did, but many women do. Because I had the support of family and friends, I was able to do something positive with a bad experience. I want to offer the same kind of support to other women and share what I have learned about physical and emotional strength.

Today, the part of my life with Michael is only a memory. While I was living it, I felt tremendous fear, despair, sadness, and anger. I believe that having that experience has made me a more humble and compassionate person, because I know how easy it is to get into such a relationship. I also know that it is possible for each of us to find the power to fill our lives with strength, conviction, confidence, and love.

INTRODUCTION

If you are the smaller one, you need to think smarter.
That's common sense.
—*a seventeen-year-old male high school student*

Now is the time for girls my age to learn we have the power and
ability to protect ourselves, and we are worth protecting.
—*Zoe Moskovitz, seventeen-year-old high school student*

In the early 1970s women became increasingly outspoken
about violence against women. They called for a national
awakening to acknowledge the prevalence of rape and sexual
abuse as an all too common experience in women's lives.
Today, after more than twenty years of working and organizing to end sexual violence, we have made significant advances. But we must ask ourselves, what have we learned in
the struggle and where are we going?

I believe we have won many battles, but we are far from
winning the war. Thanks to the hard work of men and
women throughout the country, people are becoming educated about the truths and myths of rape. We have women's
shelters and increasing numbers of government programs to
provide support services for survivors of assault, rape, and
domestic violence. The courts and the police are beginning
to empathize with women's experience and understand the

short- and long-term impact of sexual violence on women's lives. In spite of these accomplishments, sexism will probably always exist in our society, and it is quite possible that we women will have to continually fight to have our perspective publicly acknowledged and our voices heard. But sexism is not the sole cause of women's fear of and experience with violence.

I believe women's own perception of their physical inferiority contributes to the problem. Women should not blame themselves for being the victims of assault. But women must assume responsibility for their own safety, because no one else will come to their rescue. It is my experience that women generally believe (a) they are physically inferior to men and (b) they are therefore innately incapable of effectively responding to a physical threat. This belief prevents women from literally stopping the violence with their own hands. In addition, it creates an atmosphere of psychological intimidation, where actual physical violence is not necessary for men to commit acts of sexual violence. This type of gender dynamics concedes the victory to the attacker before the assault has taken place.

In every other aspect of life, women have made political, economic, and social advances through education and training. In the same way, women must learn to protect themselves from assault. Women cannot wait for society to change, for men to understand women's perspectives, and for all women to share a collective consciousness. The brutal reality of violence and its impact on women's lives is too terrible for women to deny the responsibility they have to themselves. The two most common justifications for not learning self-defense are: "Oh, I have been meaning to take self-defense, but I'm so busy right now," and "I'll never be able to learn it, I won't be any good, so why should I try?" These excuses will not help you in an attack, but educating yourself about self-defense will give you a fighting chance.

When a woman learns that she can be her own protector, it can change the way she sees herself and her world. Every woman has the capacity to learn self-defense and to gain the confidence and courage to protect herself. You don't have to be young, athletic, or coordinated. The best part of my class is watching a woman's transformation as she learns to depend on herself for her own safety. She carries herself with a pride and stature that did not exist before. In the words of one of my students:

> Before this class, I saw women, including myself, as powerless against a lot of violence. Now I feel more in control because I know what to do and how to control my situation. Women who don't take this [self-defense] course aren't helpless—they just don't know the skills.

In the first class I taught, I learned how empowering this learning process can be. It was a high school class, and in the last hour we had a group discussion about how the class affected the students' sense of confidence. Quietly and calmly, a young woman spoke out: "Last night my father beat me, and for the first time I had the courage to tell him to stop. He was not going to hit me anymore. If he did, I was going to fight back." Then she described how her father backed off and left her alone. At that moment I realized how learning self-defense can empower your mind, soul, and body so that you can face and overcome your biggest fears. I had discovered this in my own life, but no one had shared a similar experience with me.

Since that day, countless students have told me how the learning process has changed their lives. Sometimes they are even surprised by its effect:

> Taking this self-defense course has changed the way I feel about other areas of my life. You wouldn't think taking

something so small as a class that meets once a week for six weeks can make that kind of an impact. But it has. Before the class, I wasn't very happy, because I was always doing things that other people wanted me to do. Now, I am a lot less worried about what others think. I realized I don't want to change who I am or want to be. And if I am doing something that is hurting me, I have the confidence to change my situation. I can take actions to help myself.

By reading this book, you can begin the process of freeing yourself from your fear. And your self-perception will change to reflect this new power and confidence. Not only will you not be intimidated by a physical threat, other challenges in life may seem less daunting. Because if you can face an attacker then what can't you face? It may become easier for you to confidently express your opinions or to stop others from taking advantage of you. But most important, you will be able to protect yourself.

I

OUR STORIES HEARD

Sexual assault pervades every segment of our society. Women from different cultures, races, ages, and economic levels are all vulnerable. It's easy to be overwhelmed by the statistics we hear and the news we see detailing the horrendous abuse and violence numerous women suffer. It's also easy to be confused when there seem to be so many statistics and some of them contradict one another. But statistics are important for two reasons: they give us a sense of the scope of the problem, and they tell women that they are not alone in experiencing sexual assault. According to the Senate Judiciary Committee, the rate of sexual assault is increasing four times faster than the overall crime rate. The Justice Department's 1994 report on violence against women reports that between 1987 and 1991, 133,000 women twelve years and older were victims of rape or attempted rape, and approximately two-thirds of the attackers were known to their victims. In almost 90 percent of cases, attacks against women were intraracial; 21 percent of the attackers had a weapon; and less than 10 percent of the rapes involved more than one attacker.

What statistics don't give you are the people and experiences behind the numbers. This chapter presents both; it is a collection of four women's stories. As a group, they have rich and varied histories.

I asked these women to recount their experiences because they exemplify the many different ways a rape can occur and the varying responses rape survivors report as they struggle through the recovery process. They all have refused to allow the rape to destroy their sense of well-being. While their experiences continue to affect their lives, these women believe in their own strength and a positive future. They are powerfully resilient. The road they traveled was not easy, but they are imparting their stories to you in the belief that it is possible to have a good and healthy life after a rape.

Telling their stories was a cathartic experience for them. They asked themselves difficult questions, so that they in turn could share their insights with you and deepen your understanding and appreciation of the great effort required to move past the pain of a rape.

My name is Mary, and I am thirty-three years old. I was living in Miami and working as the director of an organization helping children in Central America. One night I had some friends over for pizza. When they left, I had a strong feeling that something very bad was going to happen to me that night in that house. I remember sort of brushing it aside because I had lived alone for years, and, as a woman living alone, sometimes you get eerie feelings.

It happened while I was in a deep sleep. I awoke on my stomach with someone on my back. He was choking me and saying, "Don't scream, don't scream. Who else is in this house?" I realized then that this was not a dream. There was a can of Mace inches from my bed, and as I lay there looking at it, I went into shock. But the fear was so overwhelming that I managed to lift this guy off me. He grabbed the phone and started hitting me with it. I tried to reach the Mace, but he pulled me into the next room. I couldn't see his face, because he was wearing something over it.

He raped me on the living room floor. During the rape, I left my body. I was looking from above, and then all of the sudden I would be back in my body and I would fight back. It was really strange, there was this sense of an edge. I knew just how far to push before the man became homicidal. I would fight and fight and fight, and then I would realize he was out of control and I would be still. When I was quiet, he would continue to rape me. This went back and forth many times.

I tried to talk, to convince him of the insanity of what he was doing so he would stop. I told him that my husband would be back any minute now, but he didn't pay any attention. He asked me if I was on contraception. I remember thinking, "What is this, a date we are on?" My mind couldn't adjust to what was happening. All of a sudden he became almost apologetic. He said that someone had done this to one of his relatives. I fought back, screaming, "That doesn't give you the right to do this to me!" I refused to accept that this man, besides imposing his violence on me, would also impose his twisted sense of reality on me.

At one point I got away and ran to the phone in the kitchen, but the phone was off the hook. Just as I saw a knife on the kitchen counter, he grabbed it. I thought, "This is it. I have been raped, and this is where he will kill me." But instead, he threw the knife into the living room.

He wanted me to serve him a drink. I was raging inside, but I was too terrified not to do it. All I wanted was this man to leave. He got angry with me because I had only cranberry juice and water. It was infuriating to find myself upset because I didn't have anything else and to be terrified that it might trigger him into killing me.

I started running to the front door, and there was this incredible sense of relief that I had gotten this far and had only a couple of steps more. But the door was locked. When I turned around, he had the keys in his hands. He came toward me with a smirk on his face and opened the door just a bit, but he pinned me against the wall. He started to masturbate and said, "I'm going to rape you again. You are going to get what you deserve." At that moment, we both heard a car pull up to my house. All it took was that split second for him to focus his attention on something else, and I pushed him off me and ran out of the house.

There was a police car in front of my house! I was stunned. The policeman was writing something, so he didn't see me come up. As I knocked on the window, I told myself, "Be very coherent." I told him I had been raped and the guy was still in my home. He radioed for help and then ran around the side of the house. Within seconds there were dozens of police cars in front of the house, but they lost the rapist in the woods surrounding it.

As the police combed the neighborhood, I sat with a plain-clothes officer. He told me this guy was a serial rapist. I was the seventh or eighth victim, but I hadn't heard about the rapist because I had been out of the country so much. The plain-clothes officer drove me to the hospital. I needed help, and I asked my doctor friend and my therapist to come over.

I had my medical examination, which was excruciating; the doctor was cold, explaining nothing to me. The whole thing was so clinical. I felt abandoned, but I went through with the exam because I knew I had to.

My doctor friend called my father in New York and told him I had been attacked. But besides that, I immediately took control of the situation at the hospital and acted in a very methodical manner. When I left the hospital, it was dawn. I called a few good friends and asked them to keep me company. I touched base with all the people who support and love me.

People have asked me if I have been able to trust men since

the rape. Looking back, I don't see the rapist who came into my house as a man. He was an animal. If anything, I had more difficulties with men before the rape. Afterwards I was able to see a different side to the men in my family and my male friends. I had always been very independent, and this assault gave them the opportunity to care for me and be protective.

The next day my therapist came over for two hours and we talked. But I realized quickly that he was out of his league in dealing with rape. He tried his hardest, but he really didn't know what to do. Years later he told me he was uncomfortable helping me recover from the rape, because he didn't know what it was about. Meanwhile, I couldn't sleep. I learned from news coverage that I was victim number seven. I had been on television many times because of my job, but I had always been identified, my face always on the screen. Now I was an anonymous victim. At that moment, some of what had happened started to sink in. A good friend who was with me said, "You can sleep. We are all here for you. Nothing is going to happen to you." I dozed off. Later that night my father sat in a chair next to my bed as I slept.

Even through those hard times, the only thing that kept me going was that I was not going to let the scumbag who raped me trash my life. I didn't realize that the attack was going to have a major impact on me. I needed professional help, but I particularly needed someone who knew what rape was about. I had read articles about rape, but up to that point it had seemed surreal. I wanted someone to tell me, "I have gone through it, too, and you are going to be okay."

I went to New York for two or three weeks. Time seemed to stand still. I wouldn't sleep until the sun had come up because I felt safe only during the daytime. I returned to Miami to work, but I would not set foot in that house. I asked that all my belongings and clothes be burned. I did not want anything that was part of my personal life before the rape. My parents bought me new clothes, and I picked styles completely different from those I'd worn before. I chose bold, bright colors and covered myself from head to foot.

I went back to work and I traveled, but every time I was in Miami I was terrified. The police had not caught the rapist, and I was afraid that he would find me. I became paranoid and would look at any man who was similar in shape and size, wondering if he was the rapist. Because I would not live at the house and I didn't want to be alone, I stayed with friends. But I felt added pressure as a guest in people's homes and didn't like being a burden. I resented them if they left to go out for the evening, but I also understood that I couldn't impose myself on others in this way. After two or three months, the situation was intolerable. In the past, I had never restricted my movements or felt insecure. My job's success had depended on a sense of confidence, but now I had lost that assurance and was overwhelmed with fear. I decided to leave Miami. I tried to continue my work from New York, but it was difficult; so I resigned my position.

I don't suppress the rape. I had to figure out how to have a full life and still take the rape into account. I spent a lot of time talking and crying. I went through a period of full disclosure. If the topic of violence came up at a dinner party, I would go into graphic detail about my rape. People's mouths would fall open and there would be this uncomfortable silence around the table. But every time I told my story, someone would call me afterwards and say that she had a similar experience. When I was in a group of people, I could tell who had gone through an experience like mine. That started to make me angry. There were many people out there in pain, and they were not talking about it. I knew I couldn't bottle up mine. Months went by before I could place a little more distance between the rape and myself.

I resent the sick people who, through one act of violence, can make the "walking wounded" out of otherwise healthy people. I continued to be a victim after the rape. I bought into the fear, paranoia, and loss of self-esteem. I wasn't blaming myself; I knew it was okay to feel the way I did, but I needed to reestablish my life. I wanted to walk proud again. I didn't want to spend the rest of my life cowering.

Right after the rape I went through a period of self-destructive sex. Three times I picked up men and had sex with them. I felt nothing about it afterwards. And it was something I would have been completely incapable of doing before the rape. Later, I had a relationship with a friend for protection. It scared me that I could choose a life partner for reasons of safety. I remember meeting a woman who had been raped twenty years earlier. She was in a horrible marriage because she wanted a protector.

After the rape I went through stages of losing and gaining weight. I spent a lot of time being considerably overweight because the police told me this guy had probably been watching me. I thought that if I became fat, no one would pay attention to me. I would not be seen. As if rape were about being attractive, young, or thin. That was a stupid assumption, because one of the victims was a seventy-nine-year-old woman. I felt more hatred toward the rapist for what he had done to her. I had the rest of my life to undo what he had done to me, but what about her?

I got better when I talked to people I really trusted and when I allowed myself to feel the anger and pain. The fear never quite goes away, but you learn how to manage it. After the rape I worked for two years as a volunteer for a county sexual-assault service. Just about everybody I talked to who had been raped knew it was going to happen shortly before the attack. I hear this over and over again. When are we going to start listening to ourselves? Listening to that inner voice was one of the positive things I learned from the rape.

The rape is going to affect you for the rest of your life. But the extent to which you are incapacitated is your choice.

In the long run, what I went through has become one of my most empowering experiences, although I had very little power over the situation during the rape. I was fighting for my life. There was no covert manipulation. I don't know what it must be like when you know your attacker. There is a part of me that appreciates how clear-cut my rape was, because I instinctively knew what I had to do to survive. Surviving a rape cuts away a lot of the bullshit in your life. If you are not rooted, this kind of experience forces you to communicate more honestly with yourself. Things in your life take on a different priority. You don't have time to waste anymore. I think I value my life more. I have become stronger because I have faced the reality of the violence in the world but, at the same time, have not given up caring and giving. I have realized these things coexist.

I never visualized myself as a victim. I was a human being who in the comfort of her own home had an unbelievable act of violence perpetrated on her. It was a shocking experience, but so are many other experiences in life. I think it is important that we stop seeing rape as an issue between men and women. The bottom line is that most men and most rapists have mothers who have raised them. I am also sick and tired of women not accepting responsibility for their actions and behavior. I am not saying that any woman is going out asking to be raped, but there are a lot of women doing a lot of stupid things who then turn around and say, "Poor me, no one should have to go through this." Of course no one should have to go through this; women should be able to walk down the street in the middle of the night, but that is not the reality of the culture we live in. If you are raped, you cannot continue to let your life revolve around this ordeal. If you identify with the victimhood of rape, you will be a victim the rest of your life. Let the pain out, cry, scream, deal with the stages of recovering from a rape, and then move on.

Most people assume that Mary's rapist is typical, but he is not. Approximately 5 percent of rapists are serial rapists. And he was a stranger (remember that approximately two-thirds of attackers are known to their victims). Although she faced an especially violent rapist, Mary got through the attack by keeping her head. She took a momentary opportunity to escape, thereby dispelling the myth that women can't think during times of great stress and fear.

Mary's attacker was never caught. And because sexual assault has the highest repeat rate of any felony, it is almost certain that he has raped again. Although Mary does live with the fear that he is out there somewhere, her fear has not restricted her actions. During and after the rape she demonstrated incredible presence of mind, determination, and courage.

My name is Anne. I was raped on March 7, 1992, at the age of twenty-two. I had just returned to school at the University of Maryland after working for several years. One evening I made plans to go out and celebrate the end of exams with my sister, Eileen, and a friend of hers. My sister and her friend had arrived around 9:30 or 10:00 p.m. We went to a couple of bars, and over the course of the evening I had too much to drink.

Later in the evening, Eileen's friend, who had driven, wanted to leave. A ride for us was arranged with a friend, and she left. The person giving us a ride home was the brother-in-law of my sister's roommate. Eileen had met him several times, and I knew his brother and sister-in-law fairly well. I barely remember getting into his jeep, and I passed out in the backseat shortly thereafter. The next thing I knew we were at the house, watching television in the basement family room.

I was aware of my surroundings, but not much more than that. I'd had a lot to drink. When I went upstairs to my bedroom to change, I heard a noise on the stairs and thought it was Eileen. My bedroom door was open a crack, but I quickly closed it when I heard this guy's voice. I didn't even change my clothes, because I was so startled that he had followed me upstairs. When I came out of the room, he tried to kiss me. I felt uncomfortable and told him I thought we should go back downstairs. I couldn't believe he would try to kiss me—I had barely spoken two words to him at the bar, in the car on the way home, or downstairs in the family room.

When we returned to the family room, Eileen went upstairs to change. I didn't really want her to leave, but I was not functioning well enough to ask her to stay. When she left, he and I were sitting on opposite sides of the couch. He said to me, "I never thought she would leave!" He pushed me down onto the couch as he leaned over to kiss me, and I passed out. The next thing I was aware of was Eileen screaming at him—telling him that he was raping me. He was yelling back at her, and I could hardly think because I was in so much pain.

Eileen was standing on the stairs across the room. I couldn't even look at her, because to do so I would have had to look past his face. I was terrified. To this day, if I close my eyes I can see the upholstery pattern on the couch. I couldn't move, and felt as though a part of me were floating above, watching everything that was taking place. I knew what was happening, but there was nothing I could do or say to stop him. He and Eileen continued to scream at each other. He said to her, "Don't you think she can make up her own mind? She's a big girl!" Finally, he told her that he would leave if she left the room. She didn't leave, but went up a couple of steps on the stairs so he couldn't see her. He got off me, dressed, and left. I passed out again.

Eileen called our parents to tell them what had happened. The next thing I was conscious of was my sister and mother trying to shake me awake. I was hysterically kicking and screaming, because I didn't want anyone near me and I didn't want anyone to touch me. I knew what had happened, and I felt that it was my fault. I knew I had endured a sexual assault but I was unsure what kind. It wasn't until later, when I read the legal definition of rape, that I knew what had happened to me was, by law, second-degree rape. It was second-degree rape because I was not capable of making a decision in my impaired condition.

My mother and sister took me to the hospital. Once there, we were taken to a private emergency room, where the nurses on duty began to ask questions. They asked me if I wanted to contact the police, and I said yes. The first person to arrive at the hospital was a sexual-assault volunteer, followed by a female police officer.

I spent the next few hours crying as I told my story, and retold it to the nurses, doctors, police officers, detectives, and the sexual-assault volunteer. While I was waiting to be examined, the nurses were kind—they asked me questions and checked on me as we waited for a rape kit to be delivered to the hospital. When it finally arrived, a male doctor came into the room. He positioned himself at the foot of the examination table I was on, examined me, and left. He never introduced himself, and the experience left me with the feeling that I didn't even exist, that once again I was an object.

After being released from the hospital, the female police officer and the sexual-assault volunteer accompanied me to the nearest police station. Throughout the interview, not only was I made to feel I was at fault for what had occurred, I was traumatized by the insensitive and unprofessional comments made by the investigating officer. This same detective had approached Eileen at the hospital, saying, "What if I was to touch you here? (As he touched her shoulder and leg), or what if I kissed you? Who's to say what happened?" Not only were these comments inappropriate, I feel that he made up his mind as to who was at fault before he ever interviewed me.

Everything I attempted to tell the detective was met with disbelief. He twisted what I said until it was unrecognizable. I sobbed as he tried to make me feel responsible for being raped. He asked me, "Have you ever used drugs?" When I replied that I had never used drugs in my life he said, "Well, alcohol is a drug. How come you were drinking?" He then very accusingly asked me what I had worn the night before. I had been wearing black pants, a sweater, and lace-up shoes.

My case was later closed as unfounded. According to the Federal Bureau of Investigation definition of an "unfounded" case, the rape never occurred. Ten months later, I obtained a copy of the police report and was sickened. It was colored by the investigating detective's own biases and opinions, and laid the blame for the rape at my feet. He had not heard one word of what I said.

I believe that my case was dropped because alcohol was involved. This incident could not be categorized as a violent "stranger" rape, and with the alcohol factor, it may not have seemed like a prime candidate for prosecution. I know that I am not alone. I believe that, too often, rape cases in which drugs or alcohol are a factor are not pursued, because it is feared that a jury will not convict. Having survived an attack like this, I am hurt that much of society still adheres to the view that rape is the victim's fault.

For months I was enraged. The police had told me that there was not enough physical evidence. How much evidence was needed? There had been blood all over the couch and an eyewitness (Eileen) who had never been formally interviewed. Unfortunately for me, a blood alcohol test had not been taken at the hospital. Had this been done, I believe, it would have helped my case by showing how seriously impaired I had been. The police might then have been more willing to believe what had happened.

Eventually I knew I had to start the process of putting my life, and the rape, into perspective. Since I could not ultimately make sense of the rape, I tried to focus on healing myself. I was grateful to Eileen for responding so quickly and calling our parents. If given the option, I am not sure I would have told my parents what had happened. Looking back, I'm glad I had no choice in the matter. I didn't have to hide my rape experience. And I was free to begin my healing process.

I took the following week off work and had Eileen inform my supervisors that I had been raped. I wanted them to know, because I needed them to support me throughout my struggle. My employers supported me fully. I was surrounded not only by coworkers but by very dear friends.

One of the things I needed most at this time was to feel safe. I felt as though my whole world had come crashing down at my feet, and it seemed that everything I had once hoped for, believed in, and cherished had become a pile of dust just waiting to be blown away. I had been raised believing that rape happened to other people: it happened in dark alleys and it happened to strangers by strangers. It didn't happen to people I knew, by people I knew, and it was certainly never going to happen to me.

One of the hardest things for me to accept was that I had to take responsibility for being drunk. Eventually, through a lot of painful self-examination, I began to see the difference between taking responsibility for my condition and not taking responsibility for what he did to me. I know now that I placed myself in an unsafe situation, but I was not responsible for the rape itself.

Even now, a year and a half later, I still have trouble trusting people. In some of my relationships, there comes a point where a certain amount of intimacy develops, and soon thereafter I have the almost uncontrollable urge to retreat. Although it is sometimes difficult, I have to remind myself daily to work on trust issues that are so much a part of my healing process.

It still hurts to know that there are people, sometimes friends and family members, who may not believe me when I say I have been raped. But I know that even if I have to go the rest of my life without one person believing me, I will take comfort in the truth.

Right after I was raped, there was a part of me that just wanted to die. I never want to feel that way again, and I swore I wouldn't let anyone hurt me the way I had been hurt. It was part of my defense mechanism—but it also taught me to take care of myself. I needed to learn how to become assertive, and although it was sometimes difficult, it was something I could learn.

I learned these lessons, and I learned them well. In fact, too well. There came a time when I had gotten so good at asserting myself that I pushed people away. I soon realized that I had to make some changes. I had to choose to let people into my life again. It was, and is, a process. I started out with small goals—some days I tried just to spend time with people. There were times when it seemed almost unbearable—I could hardly make myself sit because my mind, my whole being, wasn't present. I still need to remind myself: it was, and is, a process.

There are also situations, besides physical ones, in which I have had to learn how to feel more comfortable. Sometimes at work or with family and friends, I begin to feel uneasy. I call a time-out. By paying attention to how I interact with others, I can usually uncover what feelings I have that make me uncomfortable, and try to alleviate the problem. It makes me feel better to know that I can take control of the different situations I may be in.

Six months after I was raped, I began to volunteer at a

nearby sexual-assault center. At the time, I was up-front with the volunteer coordinator about my experiences. I wanted to volunteer my time partly for selfish reasons and partly for selfless reasons. I wished to give something back. I knew how important it was to have someone who believed me present during the medical examination and at the police station. I also needed to know more about rape, especially considering how sheltered my life had been.

As the months progressed, I could see myself changing. What once controlled my every waking thought soon controlled only a few minutes of my time. I learned how to process my emotions and move on. I have setbacks, but I know I can handle them by acknowledging what I am feeling, setting aside time to be alone, or finding an understanding person to talk to. The bad feelings do end. Nightmares and fear do go away. I know they no longer have the power to take over my life.

Rape recovery *can* be a growth experience. It is not easy. I know what I have experienced, what I have learned, and how I use this knowledge in my life may be different from what someone else takes from a similar experience. The most important thing I choose to remember is that *I am responsible for my own healing.* I have to hope that things can get better and I have to be willing to work to make them so. I firmly believe that for those who seek healing from a rape experience, healing is not only possible, it is *ensured.* It can get better. *It does get better.*

Anne's experience illustrates one way an unknown person may come to be trusted. Anne would never have asked for a ride home from a stranger or allowed him into her home; yet she relied on a man she had never met, because they shared mutual friends. Anne has been able to recognize what she did that made her more vulnerable to an acquaintance rape, but she rightfully does not blame herself for the rape.

Unfortunately, Anne's experience with the police made a hor-rible experience even worse. By not properly investigating her case, the detective was unprofessional and irresponsible. If a blood alcohol test had been administered, it might have shown that Anne was not physically able to give consent. Blood from the couch where the rape occurred was not collected. But the detective's biggest error was not using Eileen as a witness. It is very unusual to have a witness to a rape. But Anne did, and the police did not use her testimony to prove the merits of the case. I have consulted many police officers and district attorneys who prosecute rape cases, and they have all said that the case should not have been dropped.

Like Anne, many women have negative experiences with experts and feel further victimized by the system. Police around the coun-try are trying to educate their officers to question and protect rape survivors with more sensitivity. Anne was raped in 1992, so clearly we must continue working to improve the process rape survivors must go through when they press charges.

My name is Carolyn and I am forty-six years old. I moved to California from the East Coast in 1989 and found my dream job in northern California, running eight small busi-nesses for a savings and loan association. I loved the small town atmosphere, and I felt safe. However, I had an employee named Leo who was fixing up a cabin that I was going to move into. He was a strange young man; in fact, he made the hairs on the back of my neck stand on end, but I ignored my instincts.

I had an open-door policy with all my employees. Gen-erally, first thing in the morning the managers would come up to my house and discuss business. It was very informal. Because Leo was involved in some of the maintenance on business property, it became necessary to have him at these meetings. After about a month he started asking me about my private life. I told him that it was none of his concern, and although I became more uncomfortable around him, I convinced myself that I was being unreasonable.

In late February I took off a week to travel around northern California with a friend. When we came back, I found that Leo, who had been drunk most of the time, had done nothing on the cabin. He told me that I should not be traveling with another man, because he cared more for me. I told him there was no hope of a relationship between us. He should accept that or find another job. He went back to work.

The next week everything seemed to go well. I moved into the cabin, and I even began to feel comfortable with him because he had stopped asking about my personal life. But about a week after moving in, Leo came by the cabin around 8:00 p.m. to talk about his plans for the next day. He had been drinking, and I was afraid to have him drive home. Part of me wanted to be nice and to treat him no differently than I would any other person. The other part of me was screaming to get him out of there. I was having a real war with myself. I told him to lie down on the floor and sleep it off until the morning. Once again, I ignored my instincts.

When I got up to go to the bathroom, he grabbed my neck from behind. In shock, I asked him what he was doing. He told me I was not leaving the room. I said I had to go to the bathroom, so he let go of me. I only returned because I thought he would apologize. I told him that we were going to have a talk, but he grabbed me again. I asked him, "What do you want?" He said, "You know what I want. You know what you are going to give me. You know what you need." I said, "No, you have this all wrong. I don't need anything but for you to finish your job." "Oh no," he said. "I'm going to give you a night you will never forget." I really thought that if I could just keep him talking, he would leave me alone. I told him I had AIDS and for that reason had avoided any physical relationships. He said, "No problem. That's why they make rubbers, and I brought some."

When he threw me down on the floor, it was about 10:00 p.m. Until 6:00 a.m. he raped me four times that I know of. I retreated mentally with one thought: as long as he does not kill me, I will put the pieces back together later. But I was not going to be a willing partner. At about 6:00 a.m. I became aware of my surroundings when the phone rang. I was late to work, and one of my managers was calling to see why. I told her I had had a bad night and would be in when I could pull myself together.

I reached up to the bed, pulled a blanket down onto the floor, wrapped it around me, and told him to leave. He told me not to bother reporting the rape to the authorities, because no one would believe it was not consensual. He said that he had already told all the "boys" that we had been sleeping together for some time. He also pointed out that no one would think it unusual for his car to be parked outside the cabin all night, because he had left it there the previous week.

After he left, I sat there debating what to do. Should I take a shower? Should I call the police? I was living in a logging community of 50,000 residents, 45,000 of whom were men. There was a lot of unemployment, and I was an outsider, sent there by a big conglomerate to take over small businesses that had been foreclosed or were in bankruptcy. Pressing charges would hurt my job and my ability to deal with these people; and if I took the case to court, I did not think I would win. At the time, I persuaded myself not to go to the police. Although my first instinct was to crawl into a hole and die, I decided to get dressed, go to work, and put the experience behind me. But at work I became extremely distracted and unable to function. I was due to leave for Los Angeles the next day. I went home and I could not sleep. I found it very difficult to be in the house without every light on, and I was constantly checking the doors.

The next day I went to Los Angeles and remained there for ten days. Every time I tried to return, I would become physically ill. After the tenth day, I told my boss what had happened. I don't know what triggered his response, but he said, "If you don't go back up there within twenty-four hours, you will never work in this state again." I told him he needed to find someone to replace me but that in the meantime I would return. I called Bev, one of my managers, explained what had happened, and asked to stay with her until I could find somewhere safe to live. We finally found a gated, guarded community. I then tried to find counseling facilities, but there were very few. Rape was such a rare thing in that part of the state, no one knew how to deal with it.

I was still unsure about pressing charges. The day I returned from Los Angeles, Leo walked into my office, leaned over, and kissed me on the cheek. Although I was terrified, I fired him, and he left.

Unless someone was with me, Leo followed me for the next three weeks, stalking me everywhere I went. Several times he tried to run me off the road. At this point I was still living in denial, as if the rape did not exist.

I was raped on March 15. I went to the police in late April, and for two and a half hours told them every detail. I didn't want to press charges, because I didn't want to be in court with Leo, but I got a restraining order. The police told me I had to write down the details of the rape so that the restraining order would have some teeth to it. The judge read the complaint three times, then asked Leo if he had done these things to me. Leo said, "Well, sure I did these things to her. In fact, I did some things she can't remember." I was granted the restraining order.

The judge and the police were wonderful. Although I did not press charges, the police researched Leo's criminal record and found several outstanding warrants for his arrest. They were able to arrange it so he would spend nine years in jail. A state policeman told me that three women subsequently came forward to say that he had raped them, but they also had not pressed charges. The restraining order didn't really stop him. I had to call the police three more times before he went to jail in August.

Even though he was being sent away, it became so difficult for me to concentrate and function effectively that my work suffered and I was fired. My life had no direction. After the rape, I became resentful of men and aggressive. I was angry and sick and should have gotten therapy. Something a friend said began to make a lot of sense to me. He said, "You need to do something with this. Maybe this happened because you have the knowledge to help someone else. Maybe you can do something with this knowledge. Instead of saying why me, ask yourself how can I help."

Eventually, I moved to Las Vegas, and for the first time I opened up about the rape. I found a rape crisis center that needed counselors. When I underwent some therapy there, it was like taking the blinders off. I worked through a lot of anger and pain and finally realized that, because of the rape, I had gone from being a very outgoing, capable person to being a person who had made her life a prison. My attempt to counsel others would have been the blind leading the blind. I was terrified of life without knowing it, but the counselors let me start training. It was like group therapy: you had to open yourself up to these people. You had to trust them, or they wouldn't let you go out on the streets and let someone else bare their soul to you. I sat in that room and made sure I was in the chair that would be called on last. I listened, and I couldn't believe I was not alone. Not everyone there had been victimized, but if they hadn't, someone they loved had. I will never forget the excitement I felt after leaving. I walked out the door and I wasn't afraid.

The healing finally began at the crisis center, where there were twenty-seven people who understood. None of them said, "You should not have . . ." or "You poor baby." Instead, they looked at me and said, "I know how you feel, and it's okay to feel that way." Those words are the most important words you can hear.

I have tried very hard not to let my rape color my view of men. I have learned to respond to those little hairs on the back of my neck, and I know I will get through this. In the meantime, I continue to help rape victims understand that the rape is not their fault and that it's okay to reach out for help. I am still going through my own grieving. In the last two months I have had incredible moments of sorrow, as if someone has died. Part of me died when I was raped. Sometimes I get angry that Leo undid forty-two years of life in those eight hours, but I want my life back. When I get down to it, I really am a better person, a richer person. I am able to give the rape victims I counsel something that I did not have: someone to talk to freely and openly. No one was there for me immediately following my rape and I did not know how to reach out. I am also giving myself the gift of reaching out to someone. In my healing process, I think that is the key.

Two-thirds of rapists are known to their victims, and the way in which Carolyn was raped and her subsequent reaction to it are common. Because the fear of assault is so great for some people, they would rather live in denial and ignore their own warning signs. When this happens, it is easier for a dangerous person to take you off guard. Leo took advantage of Carolyn's refusal to listen to herself.

His strategy was typical of an acquaintance rapist, who depends on the inherent trustworthiness of the relationship. Because Carolyn knew Leo, it was easier for him to gradually break down her personal boundaries. Leo's first transgression was asking questions about her private life. In doing this he accomplished two things: he obtained information about her habits and lifestyle, and he established a relationship where he could continue to challenge her personal space. The night of the rape, he had suc-

cessfully broken down this space and manipulated her compassion (because he was drunk). He preyed on her empathy. Carolyn's experience demonstrates the ease in which women walk into a trap set up by an acquaintance rapist and the importance of having faith in your instincts about people.

My name is Christina. I do not want to be anonymous. I think that women are shamed by being raped. Shamed into losing their identity. I want people to understand that rape could happen to someone they know. Someone "ordinary." When the subject is brought up, I always acknowledge that I have been raped. People are often taken aback by my honesty and ask why I am revealing something so personal. My response to them is always the same: I have nothing to hide.

It was Friday, May 25, 1990, and I was walking home from work at about 6:00 p.m. As I walked by a building in my apartment complex, I heard loud music. When I looked up to see where it was coming from, a guy waved at me and said he wanted to talk to me. He asked if I'd like to drive to a video store with him, and I accepted. I never thought about the danger. After we dropped off the tape, we drove all over the neighborhood, which made me nervous and upset. He taunted me: "You know, you shouldn't drive around with strange men. You look kind of nervous." He tried to make passes at me, but feeling uncomfortable, I ignored it.

He dropped me off at my apartment and then called about an hour later, inviting me up to his apartment. My family and I had lived in the building for about a year. I wanted to meet people, but I had low self-esteem and no social skills. Feeling unattractive, I relished anyone talking to me. I really wanted men to pay attention to me, whether or not it was in a sexual way. So I went to see him. When I arrived, he asked me if I wanted to sit in his bedroom. Later I agreed to have sex with him. We were changing positions when he penetrated me anally. He said it was an accident, but I knew that was a lie. It was so painful I kicked him, ran out of the bedroom, and locked myself in the bathroom. He continued to ask me what was wrong, but I could hear in his voice that he knew. He snickered at me and kept saying, "Come out, come out." Even though I was naked and scared, I left the bathroom so I could put on my clothes and leave. As I was trying to dress, he kept pushing me down on the bed, saying, "Say you'll forgive me. Say it." So I said, "Fine, I forgive you." Then I left.

As soon as I walked into my house, he called, demanding, "Say that you forgive me, and come back up here. I just want to watch television with you. I won't make any passes at you. I promise." He seemed genuine, so I said fine. After I arrived, we sat down for a few minutes. Then he said that he had to finish cleaning his room and asked if I would come back with him. I went to his bedroom and I leaned against the wall. He cleaned his room for a while, and then he approached me to kiss me. I said no and turned my head. He forcefully turned my head back, pinned me against the wall, and ripped my shorts off. Then he grabbed me and threw me onto the bed and raped me. I was banging my fists on his chest, saying, "Leave me alone. Stop. Get off me." I had my door keys in my hand but was unable to jab him. When he finished raping me, he began to masturbate and ejaculated on a pile of clothes, which happened to include my underwear. All I felt was the physical pain from the earlier sodomy and the forced vaginal intercourse. He was so smug, the look on his face is locked into my memory. I didn't even know what I was doing, but I was composed. I put my clothes on, said goodbye, and left.

When I walked into my apartment that night, my mother immediately asked, "Christina, what is wrong with you?" I said nothing. I took a shower and went to bed. The next morning when I woke up, I was lying in my bed, and all of a sudden I lost my breath and started crying and shaking. It seemed as though everything in my life shut down at that moment.

I got dressed, left for work, and cried on the bus. Later that day, I went to the hospital. What affected me the most that day was my mother. She could see the pain in my face, but what hurt more than the physical pain was to see my mother wanting to help me and not knowing how.

When I told him what had happened, my father was at first very supportive and sympathetic. He never said anything about it, but he drove me to the hospital, and when he picked me up he brought me roses. That was uncharacteristic of him, because my father, a very cold man, ultimately ended up blaming me. Because I saw the guy after I was sodomized, my father believes my stupidity led to the rape. My mother thinks he needs someone to blame, but if he blames the rapist he puts the incident out of his control. If it's my fault, then he can control the situation vicariously through me by saying, "Christina's stupid. It was her fault."

I wanted to press charges, but I knew it would be difficult to prove that I was raped because there was no physical evidence. At the hospital I was interviewed by a sex and homicide detective, who happened to be a woman. I told her what happened, but during the interview I got really upset and some of my words couldn't come out. It turns out that in the police report she wrote that I was emotionally distraught and that I refused to answer any more questions. It was nothing like that. She acted as though she understood what I was saying. She never asked me to repeat myself or wanted to know more details about my rape. After the interview, they collected evidence. I had a pelvic examination with a male gynecologist, a female nurse, the sex and homicide detective, and the victim services representative in the room with me. Everyone was compassionate, but somehow I felt that I was a "victim," not a person. I started to feel humiliated by the whole process. Hair from my head and pubic area was pulled out for analysis, but I wondered if my rapist had to submit to the same examination.

The police called the guy and asked him to come down to the police station to make a statement. He said that the reason why he didn't ejaculate in me was because I was afraid to get pregnant and I asked him not to. He said that when we had consensual sex the first time, I asked him to wear a condom. Because I asked him to wear a condom the first time, it seemed like it was consensual every time (at least to him and the police). He said we had talked about seeing each other again after I left the second time.

My rapist left our apartment complex three weeks later. He had been living with his sister, because he had beaten up his girlfriend. Before he left, he would wave at me, knock on my bedroom window at night, and throw pebbles at my door to scare me. I called the detective in charge of the case and told her he was bothering me. They told him to leave me alone. I was so upset. It was driving me crazy. Then one day I walked into the shopping center across the street and his sister was there. She saw me, pointed, and screamed, "That bitch, that whore said my brother raped her. She is a liar."

Another morning when I was going to work, I saw him with a group of male friends. I tried to go another way, but they saw me and started to follow me. I was so scared. I got up to the main street and they stopped. There is no mention in the police report that he harassed me for the first two weeks after the rape. In fact, the detective wrote in the report that in her opinion I reported the rape because I had unprotected sex and feared sexually transmitted diseases and pregnancy. She also reported that I feared disgrace in my family, even though she never talked to anyone in my family.

I knew from the beginning that the guy wouldn't be prosecuted, because it was my word against his. What really bothered me was the police report. It implies that I lied and had no credibility, that the guy was victimized by me. I just want them to put down the facts as they happened. If I am the victim of another crime in the county, this report can be pulled out and used against me. My name is all over the report, but the rapist's name is blackened out.

I am not bitter, but I am angry. I do not like the way I was treated. My body was violated, and this man is free to walk around and violate someone else. For the first six months after the rape, I was a zombie. I tried to commit suicide because I just wanted my pain to end. It was the worst pain I had ever felt. Sometimes it made me physically ill. Then I became furious. I didn't talk to anyone; I just kept to myself.

Everybody was saying, "Get on with your life, Christina." But I couldn't suppress such intense emotions and pain. At first I put the episode in the back of my mind, until I was ready to deal with it. My sister is a born-again Christian, and she told me that the rape was my fault because I didn't have enough faith in God. But because I do not believe in a cruel God, her words became a catalyst for my healing process. I was angry that she would try to justify a senseless act of violence by saying it was God's will.

I survived that period of my life by keeping diaries. I call them my "writings"; they were my only outlet. My world had suddenly become unreal, and writing was the only way I could feel I was really alive. I needed to see my life in black and white. Writing was a way of sharing my emotions with myself, and it connected who I was before the rape with the person I was becoming. If I talked to people, I felt like an empty shell. I needed to save my emotional energy for myself.

I think one of the ways I helped myself was by trying to figure out what spirituality meant to me. What was faith about? What were my value systems? I believe in my inner strength, and I have hope that things will get better. I have always been stubborn, and I think that it is what pulled me through. I needed to prove to myself and my family that I could not be broken by anyone or anything.

In order for me to continue growing, I need more space between me and my family. These are the people I had shared most of my life's experiences with. But the moment I was raped, I was on my own. My family does not know the person I have become. They do not know what I went through. Perhaps it is too painful to watch someone you love go through an earth-shattering experience if you are emotionally unstable yourself. In no way do I excuse my family's reactions, but understanding them enabled me to forgive them.

I am a much happier and more contented person now. I think the Christina that was raped is a reminder of what I don't want in my life. Every time I put myself in a dangerous situation or I am not listening to my instincts, I remember the fact that I was raped.

I am proud of the fact that I survived this experience. I have learned things about myself and the world because of it. It could either break my resolve or strengthen it. I don't know if I will ever be raped again, but I do know that no one can ever take my soul. And my soul is too precious to give up without a good fight. I will never give up control of my body and mind to anyone ever again.

Non-consensual intercourse is still rape, even if the woman made some poor choices or had previously agreed to have sex. Some people would read Christina's story and say, "She was asking for it," or "This can't be rape, and it would never happen to me like that, because I would be able to see what was coming." Some kinds of rape are easier to doubt than others, but that doesn't mean they didn't occur. The fact is that a woman was terribly hurt, and the rapist was not held accountable for his actions.

Christina was at a point in her life where she wanted to take risks, but she didn't have the skills to recognize the danger she was walking into. This is the dilemma that continually arises for young women. In order to grow up, they will naturally test themselves in different situations. Inevitably, some of these situations are dangerous. I have spoken to many women who look back on their youth and are grateful they are still alive. I don't think anyone cannot remember doing something or making a decision that, in hindsight, was incredibly dangerous.

I don't think we should discourage young women from experimenting with different life choices, because they will make their own decisions anyway. Being an adult means taking responsibility for the consequences of your actions. As a society, I believe we must give these women the skills to make good decisions.

2

ENTERING THE VOID:

AN INTRODUCTION TO SELF-DEFENSE

I believe that success in life is achieved by recognizing different challenges and adapting and responding to them appropriately. Effective women's self-defense relies on the same abilities. Because each attacker and each victim is an individual, the dynamics of an assault will always be different; a guaranteed strategy against a specific attack does not exist. However, I can guarantee that if you educate yourself about the nature of the interaction between women and their attackers, you will be better prepared to stop potential attackers and to respond more effectively to every aspect of the attack.

As the course I teach progresses, many students are amazed by how clearly they can strategize while under attack. Some people initially believe they will not be able to think during the simulated attacks (class exercises where the student practices techniques with an instructor wearing protective gear). You do not have to learn physical self-defense to be better prepared for an attack. Thinking, strategizing, and adapting to situations as they change are as important as physical self-defense skills. Self-defense means sending the right body and verbal signals before the attack. During an attack it means empowering yourself by making decisions, not giving up, and knowing you can think your way through the experience. You can respond to assaults effectively.

Body Language

Body language communicates how comfortable you feel about yourself. In self-defense, effective body language conveys a relaxed sense of confidence. If you doubt that body language works, think about it from the attacker's perspective. If you were a man who attacks women, whom would you go after? A woman who appears weak, afraid, or powerless. An attacker does not want to pick a confident woman, because he attacks to demonstrate control and power. Because such a man may be insecure to begin with, he must search for a woman whose behavior and/or actions would satisfy his needs. An attacker does not assault women who present a possible challenge. He picks a sure bet. If you can convince him that you are not that woman, he will look elsewhere. And, unfortunately, he can easily find a woman who fits his criteria.

The first phase of an attack is often called the "targeting" stage; the attacker is searching for a victim. During this phase, confident and relaxed body language is critical. I see many women after work with their heads down, staring at the sidewalk. This body language clearly communicates two things: first, the woman is exhausted and too tired to protect herself; second, the woman is staring at the ground because she is afraid to look anyone in the eye or she is simply not aware of her surroundings. Either way, she is an easy target. Officer Michele Carson of the Cheverly, Maryland, police department has this advice:

People have been raised to be so passive . . . Have a dare attitude. Get rid of that "I'm a victim of my demanding boss and ungrateful kids, and I'm a wimp" look. Think about the way you carry yourself. It does not have to be a negative posture; you can project an air of confidence. As you walk down the street, the physical and mental signal you want to send to a potential assailant is: "Don't even think about it. I am not something to be trampled underfoot."

There are ways to walk more safely. Keep your head up, look ahead, and drop your shoulders (do not hunch them). Walk with a relaxed step (not too long or too short), and keep your hands out of your pockets. Compare these two images in your mind: the woman looking down at the ground and the one just described. Who is an easier target? Who appears vulnerable? These changes are small, but they make an enormous difference.

The way attackers choose their victims is similar to the way predators choose their prey. They always go after the sick, isolated, young, or old because they are an easy kill. Consider potential attackers as animals that will prey on you if given the opportunity. If you look strong, alert, and healthy, you have a much better chance of being left alone.

Verbal Self-defense

The second stage, or testing phase, of an attack usually involves some kind of verbal communication. There are two different kinds of verbal self-defense in response to a threat from an attacker. The first, and most common, is assertive verbal self-defense. Assertive self-defense is used when the attacker is unarmed or does not have physical control of you to the extent that fighting back would cause you greater injury. It is simply an extension of your body language: you are verbally communicating that you refuse to be seen as a victim. The second, cooperative verbal self-defense, is used when the attacker has a weapon or is holding you in a way that makes it useless to fight back at that moment. Hopefully it will make the attacker relax so that he will feel in control. You may use cooperative verbal self-defense if you decide that you don't want to fight back. Or you may want to use it to trick the attacker. When he lets up, you may have the opportunity to escape or physically fight back. For example, you might say, "I'll do whatever you want, but please let go of me."

In any kind of sexual assault, the attacker has two objectives. First, he must control you so that he can sexually assault you. Second, he gauges your strength by observing your response to his harassment or threats. If the attacker is unarmed, verbally threatens you, and sees you are weak during this phase, he can be fairly confident that he can continue the assault with little resistance.

Verbal self-defense is used in all types of sexual assault, whether by an acquaintance, a date, or a stranger. Your goal is to match the conflict level with a strategy and a tone of voice. Listen to what the attacker is saying and how he is saying it. Ask yourself how violent you think this person is. For example, you are walking down the street and a man says, "You're so cute, honey, wanna come home with me?" Most likely, you have met with this before and you walked away annoyed but safe. You already have these coping skills. You want to avoid a fight if at all possible. In the situation described above, walking away is an appropriate response. He has not touched you and he could be harmless. But what happens if this person comes closer to you or continues the verbal harassment? You need to change your strategy and clearly communicate your intentions. Look him in the eyes and slowly, confidently say, "Leave me alone," "I don't want any trouble; your problems have nothing to do with me," or

"Get away from me." Do not mumble or use a pleading tone. You are commanding him to leave you alone.

Recently I had a student who was attacked a few days after she had taken her first self-defense class. She was sitting on the bus next to a man, and he started to ask her questions. She responded politely, but got up and moved to another seat when he tried to place his hand on her knee. When she sat down in the other seat, he followed her but remained standing closely behind her. A while later, at her stop, she got off, making sure to stay close to other people. She looked for the man but did not see him get off. As soon as she turned the corner and was on her own again, the man from the bus grabbed her. She immediately screamed, "Get off me! Leave me alone!" He turned and ran away.

This is a good example of assertive verbal self-defense effectively changing the dynamics of the assault in the woman's favor. She took the power away from the attacker by standing up for herself. Confident body language and verbal self-defense can be used in every situation. However, there are some common situations where more specific strategies can be applied.

Safety Tips

The response of most women after an attack is "I can't believe it happened to me." This belief is one of the fundamental reasons why women are unable and unwilling to recognize danger. Why do women believe this when they see and hear stories of rape every day? Because the more distance they can place between the stories and themselves, the safer they feel. When they are attacked, they are caught off guard and feel powerless to stop the attacker. On the other hand, women can't be paranoid and suspicious of everyone. A balance must be achieved so that women can enjoy life while being realistically prepared.

THE STREET

Walk confidently, and trust your instincts. Keep your eyes forward, shoulders relaxed, and take strong but not unnaturally large steps. If you see someone who makes you feel uncomfortable, trust your feelings. Your options depend on the amount of time and space between you and the individual. If there is more than twenty feet between you, cross the street. If you cannot cross, walk in a direction that leaves more space between you when you pass. As you are passing each other, look at his hands. If he does intend to attack, his hands are going to be his weapons, not his eyes. If you like to look in people's eyes, that's fine, but be sure not to do so in a confrontational, aggressive manner.

If you are physically attacked, scream. Screaming serves two purposes. It calls attention to you, and it makes clear to others that you are being attacked. (However, do not count on other people to come to your rescue; it rarely happens.) Equally important is that the scream counteracts the natural tendency to gasp when a person panics. Gasping makes it very difficult to breathe, and not being able to breathe contributes to the overwhelming sense of helplessness that occurs in the first moments of an attack. It is also important to scream with an authoritative tone. Unfortunately, when women become nervous or frightened, their voices tend to have a higher pitch, which communicates fear and powerlessness. So when you scream, scream from your diaphragm, not from your throat.

Practice screaming, and scream whatever comes naturally to you. If you are attacked, you do not want to think about what you should be screaming, so prepare some possible options. I tell my students to scream "NO!" because it can act like a jump start for your body and mind. However, you do not have to scream a word. Use any sound that is natural to you at the time.

BEING FOLLOWED

I bring this up because many of my students have been followed. Although it's frightening, the good news is that assertive verbal self-defense works very effectively. In fact, the combination of being aware of your surroundings and then facing the person is usually all you have to do. The following two stories show that sometimes it's better to escape without the verbal confrontation and sometimes you need it.

Six months after graduating from our program, a woman and her friend (who had not taken the class) were walking in a very crowded area on a Sunday morning. The first woman noticed that a man was following them but always remained about five feet behind them. A few moments later, she realized he had taken out a bicycle chain and was wrapping it around his hands. She also realized that they were walking away from the streets full of people. She immediately grabbed her friend and walked to the nearest open populated building, a restaurant. Her friend had no idea that the man was behind them.

Another student always rode the subway home from work. She noticed a few nights in a row that she was seeing the same man every time she got off the elevators and that he was following her for a few blocks. On the third night, he followed her again, but this time she abruptly turned around, faced him, and screamed, "Stop following me right now!" He ran away.

PARKING GARAGES AND GETTING
INTO YOUR CAR

Parking garages are filled with potentially dangerous situations. You are at greater risk here, because you are often alone and easily isolated. The overall rule is to defend yourself only when your body is under attack. If the attacker wants something you have—your purse or car, for example—give it up (but don't give him your keys unless he asks for them). Whatever he wants, you should try to get away as quickly as you can. I have often been asked how to determine whether the attacker wants you or what you have. To give yourself more time, I recommend that you throw whatever you have on the ground as far away from you as possible. If he wants you, he'll obviously continue moving toward you after he picks up your money.

The more you know about your surroundings, the better you will react. When parking your car, try to avoid parking next to vans with sliding doors. This might be difficult and inconvenient, but it could be well worth the effort. Before you get out of the car, look for exit doors or garage attendants. Take the time to do this, because women who are attacked and try to run away often run to places that only make the assault easier for the attacker. You want to run to safety, not just away from danger. Take the keys out of the ignition and place the key that locks the door firmly between your thumb and index finger. This way you can lock the door quickly and have a readily available weapon.

If someone comes up to you and demands the keys, throw them away from you and run toward the escape routes you previously planned when you entered this environment. If the person goes after you instead of the keys and you have not been able to gain sufficient distance to be safe, face the person, look him in the eye, and in a strong, confident voice use your verbal self-defense. You want to face him because if he catches you, there is a strong possibility that you will be thrown to the ground. Also, facing him is the last thing he expects, and surprise is a very effective weapon. You are transferring the power from him to you. Remember, holding your ground and refusing to be seen as a victim usually stops the attack.

WALKING FROM/TO YOUR CAR

Have your keys out. Walk in the same way that you would on the street. If you are holding bags that weigh you down and restrict your movement, increase your awareness, because you are more vulnerable. Continue to look forward, but be very careful of the large pillars in parking lots where a person can easily hide. Use your peripheral vision to see any unusual movement around you. If you are approached, use your verbal self-defense strategies. If the person continues the attack, drop the bags quickly and scream.

GETTING INTO THE CAR

Before getting into the car, look in the backseat or anywhere a person can hide in your car. When everything is clear, get inside and lock the door behind you.

When I was living in Los Angeles, there was a man who attacked women when they were getting into their cars. His method was to hide under the car, grab the woman's ankles, and force her to the ground. After I heard about this, every time I returned to my parked car I would stop about twenty feet from it and look underneath it. I always thought this was foolish because I was leaving myself blind to anyone else who might attack me. So this is what I do now. About ten feet from the car I look around to see who is there. If I feel safe, I take a quick look under the car. If someone grabs you in this way and you are caught off guard, as soon as you feel something on your foot or ankle, lift your free leg, stomp it on the person's hand, and run to safety.

WALKING TO/FROM THE OFFICE AND HOME

There are many women who have been attacked walking to and from the office and home. Not surprisingly, adult women I meet in seminars and classes frequently tell me how vulnerable they feel. To increase your safety, keep your keys in your hands at all times so you can use them for self-defense (see page 72). Use the body language strategies discussed above. But most of all, make safety your primary thought. It is natural to leave the office or home with ten things on your mind, and being aware of your surroundings is not one of them. But for those few minutes, take care of yourself by concentrating on your safety.

ASKING AND RECEIVING INFORMATION/ GIVING DIRECTIONS

The two most critical components of a fight, regardless of the sex of the participants, are timing and distance. In protecting yourself, you have to be sure that a safe distance is maintained between you and a potential attacker. A safe distance is usually defined as the length of your arm plus the arm length of the attacker (usually a total of five or six feet). When someone asks for directions, whether one or both of you are in a car, make sure you maintain this distance. Any information can be transferred from a safe distance. Do not let anyone lean into your car to give you information, and do not roll your window completely down. If the person is coming too close, tell him to back up. You do not have to be rude. For example, you could say, "Would you please not come any closer," or "That's okay, you can stay there. I can hear you from here." This way you are establishing boundaries for yourself and the stranger. If he crosses this boundary, you have more reliable information concerning his intentions, and you are better prepared to respond.

JOGGING PATHS AND PARKS

Both jogging paths and parks are places where women are often alone or easily isolated from other people. Above all, please do not wear headsets. If you have a dog or can borrow one, I strongly encourage you to run with a dog. They are a wonderful deterrent. If you are running on a path, do not automatically assume that the person who means harm is the one with the dirty or unkempt appearance. Often women are surprised by attackers who wear clean clothes and appear well groomed.

I recently heard a story that demonstrates the importance of running *to* safety and not just away from danger. A woman in her junior year of college was running on a campus trail during an early weekend morning. As she ran, she passed a clean-cut man in his late twenties who was running in the opposite direction. He doubled back and attacked her from behind. She was able to fight him off and immediately ran off the path to escape him. Unfortunately, she did not think about where she was running. By running off the trail she placed herself in greater danger: she became lost and was easily found by the attacker a few minutes later. Now that she was even further isolated and panic-stricken, he was able to rape her and escape without anyone seeing him. If you need to run away, never stray from the path or from a location where people are more likely to be.

A park presents a similar environment and similar dangers. Do not arrive there totally fixated on who does or does not look suspicious. You are there to enjoy yourself. However, if you see someone who gives you an uneasy feeling, recognize it and increase your awareness. You must train yourself to be alert. In this way you can enjoy life while being your own best protector. At first, as you try to incorporate these safety tips into your daily schedule, you may feel paranoid. Give it time.

HOME

It may surprise you to know that women over thirty-five are most vulnerable to physical assault in their home. This is because as women get older they go fewer places; they tend to shuttle between the office, home, gym, and grocery store.* Obvious safety tips here include inspecting your windows. Do you have any that can be opened from the outside? How resistant are they to intrusion? Are the locks on your door easy to jimmy? Most attackers enter by persuading you to open the door or by kicking the door until they break the screws holding the deadlock in the door frame. If you want to check your home's security, try to break into your own home. If you can get in, you can be sure that someone else can as well.

If you are home at night and hear someone breaking into the house, assume that the attacker is there to attack you, not to burglarize your home. Robbers know that most people are not at home during the day, so they choose this time to steal. A person who breaks in at night knows that people will most likely be there, so there's a good chance that he is breaking in to attack you. If you do hear someone, don't wait in bed, paralyzed by fear. Call the police immediately. If you have a

---

* Ronet Bachman, *Violence Against Women: A National Crime Victimization Report,* January 1994, U.S. Department of Justice, Bureau of Justice Statistics, NCJ-145325, p. 3.

cordless phone, preprogram the emergency number and leave the phone by your bed. You should prepare an escape plan, such as you might have thought about for escaping a fire. But no matter how your home is laid out, you should call the police first.

ALARMS, MACE, AND PEPPER GAS

Personal safety devices are becoming an increasingly popular choice for women who are concerned about assault. In my opinion, utilizing your mind and body for personal safety is best overall, but there are certain circumstances where safety devices can be useful. Alarms and stun devices are my least favorite. I am referring to the portable alarms that usually look like Walkmans and to the stun guns that shock a person when touched. Alarms are useful in three situations: if you are the victim of a car-jacking; if a stranger approaches you from a distance; and if an intruder tries to enter your house. In these scenarios, I believe the alarm can be an effective deterrent. I don't like it, because its advertisements imply that when it goes off, people will come to the rescue. I don't think they will, because it sounds like a car alarm which people ignore all the time. And a high, loud sound, while annoying, cannot incapacitate. Stun guns are dangerous because you have to touch the attacker for it to work. And if you can touch him, he can hit you. This wouldn't be so bad if the women using them were trained in self-defense, but most women aren't. Mace is okay, but it has limitations. Police officers who have used it report some failures. Mace doesn't seem to work if the attacker is on an amphetamine. So if you are going to carry a personal safety device, I suggest pepper gas in a cannister with a recessed button, which prevents accidental firing. Don't buy one with a safety latch, because the attack will occur too quickly for you to adjust it. However, pepper gas is only effective if you understand when it is most appropriate to use it. I like it for running and other outside activities (if you don't have a buddy or a dog). I also like it for walking from one place to another. For example, between your car and the office, grocery store, or home. You have to be ready and willing to use it. Don't buy it and keep it in your purse. Hold it in your hand, ready to fire.

GUNS

Many adult women, especially those who live alone, ask me if I support keeping a gun in the home for self-defense. In almost all circumstances, especially if there are children, I do not. In particular, I do not think it is a good idea to have a handgun. But I want to give an overview on guns so that you will be better informed on the issue in general. Far too many women are intimidated by the whole subject and get information from organizations and people who may not have women's best interests in mind.

The most common guns used in homes are handguns and shotguns. Each one has its advantages and disadvantages. Handguns are compact and fit into your nightstand, and the ammunition can be stored separately but kept ready for quick loading. The two most common types of handguns are revolvers and semiautomatics. Revolvers hold the bullets in a drum (which typically holds six bullets), and only one bullet is lined up with the barrel at any given moment. As the hammer is drawn back, the drum rotates and lines a new bullet up with the barrel. The advantage of a revolver is that it is mechanically simple and has intrinsic safety features. It can't jam, and it can be stored half-cocked, meaning the hammer is partially pulled back so that it is not touching the bullet. Therefore, a sudden blow to the gun, like dropping it, will not fire the bullet. Its greatest disadvantage is that it holds only six rounds, so it has limited firepower. If you want to load a revolver rapidly, you can get a speed loader. This is a device that holds six bullets in the exact configuration of the drum. When you want to load the gun, drop the drum out, slide the bullets in, and turn the knob on the speed loader to release the bullets. Return the drum home. Revolvers are most popular with inexperienced users.

In a semiautomatic, each time a bullet is fired, the spent bullet case is discarded and a new bullet is loaded into the chamber automatically. The bullets are kept in a magazine, also called a clip, that can be removed from the gun. When you want to load the gun, you place the magazine in the gun, pull back and release a slide, and you're ready to fire. The semiautomatic has two disadvantages: it is a more complex machine, so more things can go wrong; and it can jam. Jamming occurs when the gun either fails to completely eject the spent bullet case, a new round is not loaded, or something, like a piece of clothing, interferes with the operation of the slide. Jamming is unlikely to happen if you keep your gun clean.

The major disadvantage with any handgun is that you have to be a very good shot to use it effectively, because it discharges a single projectile each time you fire. If your hand is shaking because you are nervous facing someone who has broken into your house, you will most likely miss. To make matters worse, a bullet travels with a great deal of power and speed—enough to easily pierce most walls and kill innocent people in other rooms or nearby houses.

Shotguns fire multiple projectiles in a spread pattern with each shot. They spray the ammunition over a greater area. You don't have to be as accurate as with a handgun. You just point the shotgun in the direction of the target. There are three varieties of shotguns. A breech-loading shotgun is loaded by opening the gun where the barrel meets the receiver. Depending on whether it is single- or double-barreled, you load one or two rounds. It is a very simple operation but has limited firepower. A pump-action shotgun is similar to a semiautomatic handgun but doesn't eject and load bullets by itself. You reload by pumping the front grip once for each round. A pump-action shotgun usually holds three to eight rounds in the magazine. A semiautomatic shotgun reloads by itself. Both pump action and semiautomatic shotguns look double-barreled, but the lower barrel is really a nonremovable magazine. Such weapons present a serious problem for people with children, because having a nonremovable magazine requires that the gun be stored loaded if it is to be used on short notice. In general, this is the problem with all guns when children are going to be anywhere near them. To keep them out of the reach of children, you need to store the gun and ammunition separately, but then you can't load the gun quickly for use in an emergency.

Some people prefer a sawed-off shotgun because it is meant for firing in close quarters. It has an even wider spread—so there's less chance you'll miss. You should use buckshot as ammunition in a shotgun. Buckshot has enough impact and power to stop the attacker; but its speed and energy decrease quickly, so it doesn't go through walls like a bullet. Buckshot also has a range of approximately three hundred yards, while a bullet can have a range of up to a mile. An additional benefit of a shotgun is the sound of it chambering. According to Rob Shuster, a former police officer, "The sound of a pump action shotgun is a universal deterrent."

If you do decide to buy a gun, educate yourself about all the options. Do not think you can buy one, load it, and be safe. You need to be trained and to practice regularly. But even so, practicing in a controlled environment is not comparable to using a gun in a real situation. You should assume that if you shoot someone, you accept the likelihood of their death. Don't wait until a life-or-death situation arises before asking yourself if you are prepared to make this decision.

Training will not prepare you for facing an attacker, possibly in the dark, with your family members sleeping close by.

Who Is Going to Attack Me?

You probably have an image of a rapist in your mind. When I talk to women, they frequently tell me that they imagine an insane man jumping out of the bushes. Beyond that, have you ever thought about it in greater detail? What kind of person would you be dealing with? Angry? Sad? Insane? Calm? Intelligent? Calculating?

To better prepare your self-defense strategy, it helps to have a personality profile of the attacker. From now on, depersonalize the attacker. View him as a personality type, not another individual. As Mary said in chapter 1, her attacker was an animal, not a person. Like a predator, an attacker preys on a woman who tends to empathize. You are defending yourself against the behavior, not the person. Do not feel sorry for him. If someone assaults you, he's made a choice to violate you in the most fundamental way. He does not have the right to attack, but you have the right to protect yourself.

STRANGERS

An appropriate response to a threatening stranger depends on how violent you perceive him to be. A man who makes sexual assaults can have many motivations, or the degrees of his anger may vary. Understanding him as quickly as possible is essential for your safety and possible escape. I divide the stranger into three personality types: insecure, self-centered, and sadistic. If you are ever attacked, I suggest that your response strategy include deciding which personality your attacker fits. Keep in mind that I have to generalize. As every person is different, the following can only provide a framework on which to base your decisions.

The Insecure Rapist   The insecure rapist attacks to overcome his own fears of inadequacy. He acts to regain control and power in a world where he feels he has none. Some clues to identify the insecure rapist: Does he seem frightened? Does he sound unsure of himself or nervous? Is he denigrating himself and seeking sexual approval? The insecure rapist will not usually threaten to hurt you; his primary objective is control. He may try to reassure both of you that this is an enjoyable experience. Examples of what he might say are "Do you like me?" and "I'm not going to hurt you." It is not uncommon for this type of attacker to ask for your phone number or for a date after the assault.

Of all the types, the insecure rapist is most likely to be stopped with only assertive verbal self-defense, because your will to deter the attack is stronger than his to carry it out. The more confident you are, the better. Verbal self-defense strategies include using a tone of voice that is firm and clear but not angry. Examples are "I want you to leave me alone now" and "I cannot help you. Leave me alone." You may decide to empathize with him as part of your strategy, but remember to state plainly what you want. The following story shows that some insecure attackers are not committed to the attack if the woman stands up for herself.

A friend of mine was walking to her car in a residential neighborhood of Washington, D.C. As she crossed the street, she heard someone calling her from a distance. Even though the person was about a hundred feet away, she realized she did not recognize him, and he was drunk. She headed back to the house, but the man succeeded in catching up with her before she could get inside. He had positioned himself so that there was no way she could return to the house or get to the car without walking by him. At this point she noticed that he was bloody around the nose and had a fat lip. He screamed at her, "I'm going to beat the shit out of you." She responded, "Get the hell away from me. Your problems have nothing to do with me, so just keep moving!" As soon as she said this, his hands fell to his sides. He took a step back, and mumbled something she could not hear. Seeing that this strategy made the attacker hesitate, she repeated her commands until he left, saying, "Yeah, right. Peace."

The Self-centered Rapist The self-centered rapist is a man who cannot see a woman as his equal. He easily feels threatened and challenged by women. To him, women are objects to be used when and where he wants. The strategy against the self-centered rapist is difficult because he can be highly unpredictable. However, knowing this gives you power, and you need to use it to your advantage. The first strategy is to use assertive verbal self-defense, because any weakness further entrenches his perception of you as a helpless woman. If you react weakly, he will believe he is justified in raping you or that you wanted it in the first place. You can shatter his fantasy of your powerlessness by refusing to be seen as a victim. If you present a strong front, he may decide that it is not worth the effort. When you are speaking to him, look directly at him and speak with an authoritative tone. Suggested things to say: "Leave me alone now!" "Go away. Do not bother me!" If he laughs, do not break down. He is trying to ridicule you and make you feel powerless. Once he makes you feel that way, he has won the battle.

This strategy may not work if he begins the assault by physically controlling you in a way that is dangerous for you to resist. Assertive verbal self-defense may well be interpreted as a challenge to his power, and his response may be to escalate the conflict into a physical assault. This person presents such danger to you because it is difficult to predict his response. The most important thing to remember is that it is your

judgment call and your decision. When you use your cooperative verbal self-defense, say things that will calm him
down. If you see an opportunity to use physical self-defense
(see chapter 3) or to escape, take it. If you believe that you
can't back up your words with physical actions, make a decision that you believe will cause you the least pain and suffering. You can also try to negotiate with the attacker. Survival
is the primary goal. If the alternatives are being beaten and
raped or being raped, I would choose the latter. Most of all,
have confidence in yourself to make the decisions necessary
to survive.

The following story happened to me. While you read it,
think about the safety tips and strategies I have described and
how they suit the following scenario. I believe this incident
illustrates how to be aware of a potential attack and stop it
before it starts.

I had spent the morning in a library in suburban Maryland
and decided to take a lunch break. I checked out a book, *The
Rape Survivor's Handbook,* and went outside. There was a
park next to the library and a supermarket across the street.
As I walked through the park, I noticed four men in a group.
I felt targeted, but I did not know for what. I went to the
supermarket, bought my lunch, returned to the park, found
a table, and sat down. Five minutes later I looked up to see
one of the men circling me but maintaining about a twenty-
foot distance. I went back to my lunch but concentrated on
any surrounding activity. Within a minute the man sat down
on the other side of my table. After looking at the book cover,
he asked: "Have you ever been raped?"

What was going on? First, this man was invading my
personal space (he was uncomfortably close to me). And he
was asking me an inappropriate and intimidating question
to assert control. As he spoke to me, I made a mental checklist
of his potential danger. I estimated his height and weight,
and noted facial characteristics and scars. He did have a scar

running across his neck. This increased my concern. I asked myself if he was drunk or high, and decided he was not. I looked for weapons and saw none. I casually looked around to see my escape route, other people around me, and the location of the other three men. When I completed this checklist I closed my book as if to leave. As soon as I did this, he asked me if he could walk me back to the library. Looking straight into his eyes, I said in a very firm voice, "No, you cannot. I want you to leave." He told me again that he was going to walk me to the library, and I said once more, "No, you're not walking me back. You are going to leave." When he left and there was a safe distance between us, I got up and walked back to the library. Five hours later, when I left for the day, I walked to my car completely focused on the possibility of his reappearance. He was nowhere to be seen and I was safe.

It was not necessary in this situation to know his exact intentions. My principal concerns were his invasion of my space, his opening line, a scar on his throat, and his asking me to walk back with him. These were clues. I felt that I had been singled out. When I returned to the library, I knew I was safe temporarily, but as soon as I left the building I immediately focused on the possibility of danger.

The Sadistic Rapist   Though the least common, this attacker is the most dangerous. He attacks women as an outlet for the rage he feels toward other things in his life. Releasing anger is his primary goal; sex is not. One of the ways to identify this type is that the verbal and/or physical abuse is disproportionate to the amount needed to control you. Use cooperative verbal self-defense to try to de-escalate his hostility if he poses an immediate physical threat to you. You do not want to say anything that raises the level of conflict, because he will respond with increased violence. Possible things to say are "What is making you angry?" or "Do you want to talk about it?" Your success depends on your ability to calm him down.

Never let anyone, especially the sadistic attacker, remove you from the initial place where you are accosted. If you are removed, you will be isolated from others, and his feeling of invincibility and freedom will increase. In a situation like this, you should fight back no matter what. There are other circumstances in which I recommend fighting back. If the attacker has anything that binds (such as rope, duct tape, or wire), fight back immediately, because it is considerably more difficult to negotiate or control this situation when you are physically restrained.

If you do not think you can fight, here is some advice. Do not panic. You can defend yourself. Your will to survive is stronger than his will to hurt. The moment before you strike back, visualize your confidence, power, and strength as a collective force, and mentally commit yourself to the struggle. Think of all the people in your life who have given you support, nurture, and love. Imagine them fighting with you. Their strength adds to your own, and you will be fighting back together.

ACQUAINTANCES

The most current research shows that two-thirds of assaults against women are committed by acquaintances.* However, the word *acquaintance* describes a wide range of relationships. A person you see on the subway or bus once a week on the way to work and exchange hellos with is an acquaintance. A man who regularly cleans your gutters is an acquaintance. So is a good friend or a fellow employee. Because acquaintances include relationships with various degrees of intimacy, it can

* Bachman, *Violence Against Women,* p. 3.

be difficult to recognize a potential attack and respond appropriately.

If you feel that an assault is going to take place or has already begun, think about what you know of this person. Using the personality descriptions illustrated above, decide which one he best matches. If you know him well, you may be uncomfortable being assertive and direct. But it is absolutely necessary to understand his intentions and his resolve in carrying them out. If you do not know him well, carefully watch his response to your actions and words. Again, trust your gut feelings. Even if you barely know him, you know something. Does he blame others easily for his own misfortune? Have you seen him angry before? If so, was he violent? In the past, did he talk over you or not listen to you? Information is power. Use it to your advantage.

DATE RAPE

It is vitally important to your safety to be able to recognize a potentially abusive or actively abusive relationship. Oddly enough, it can be difficult to recognize danger. Especially for young women who are forging their personal identity, values, and boundaries, understanding abuse is often confused with a maze of other feelings, like insecurity, fear, and love.

In a dating situation the rule of thumb is to know what your personal boundaries are before you go on a date. Sit down ahead of time and think: "What do I feel comfortable doing with a person on a casual date?" "At what point during sexual intimacy do I feel uncomfortable?" "If I do feel uncomfortable, what are some things I might say to clearly communicate my feelings?" When you are clear about these things, make a pact with yourself to stand by them. If you know your limits before you are in an intimate situation—

when you may not be thinking as clearly as you might like —you can rely on an established set of personal guidelines to assist you.

The dating situation can be very confusing, because a number of factors combine to make both people's intentions and desires unclear. We are still raised to repress our sexuality. Men are often raised within a cultural framework that values sexual intercourse over other types of intimacy. This does not mean that men are unable to stop themselves once their "sex switch" turns on. They, as human beings, have been blessed with the ability to think and listen to verbal communication and are ultimately responsible for their own behavior. However, in a dating situation, both people may be unsure of what they want or about how to say it. A woman may be sexually aroused but not want sexual intercourse. She may feel uncomfortable asserting herself or fear that she will be rejected if she doesn't give in. Or, unfortunately, she may be vulnerable to emotional and physical intimidation. Together, all these components interact to create the dynamics of date rape.

When you go on a date you are placing yourself in a potentially dangerous situation, because our cultural values encourage men to believe in their inherent right to initiate sexual intercourse and to make women feel confused about their sexuality and their right to say no. Even if the man you are with does not believe in men's right to dominate women, some part of his interaction with you is based on these cultural beliefs. This belief makes it more difficult for him to listen and respect what a woman is saying, especially when he may see sex on the horizon. It also makes rape an easier act to commit and deny.

Keeping this in mind, you have some power as long as you know when you can most effectively use it. Up to the moment when a man forces sexual intercourse, you have certain responsibilities to yourself. Sex is dangerous, and to ignore that fact places you at greater risk for an assault. Here are some choices you have to make:

1. Are you going to have intoxicants? If so, how much?
2. After the date is over, are you going to enter this person's home or allow him in yours?
3. How well do you have to know someone before you feel comfortable being alone with him?

Overall, throughout the date you have the power to set and communicate guidelines for yourself and your date.

No matter what precautions a woman takes during a date, the result can be nonconsensual sex. Without physical self-defense training, and sometimes even with it, a woman can be overpowered by a man. Why? Because most men are physically stronger than women, and we live in a world where men are given the power to initiate sexual intercourse. From my perspective you have the responsibility to protect yourself and act in your best interest. But if you do this and the man you are with does not respect your decisions or your right to make them, you are not responsible in any way for his actions.

Usually date rape occurs within the home (either the woman's or the man's). Often men report that they must persuade women to have sexual intercourse because women are taught to "play hard to get." Your successful verbal self-defense in this situation depends on dispelling this fantasy. Telling the man that you do not want to have sex by saying things like "I really don't know if we should do this," "Not now, can't we wait?", or "I really like you but I'm not sure" is not effective. All these statements can be misconstrued as meaning that you need a little more urging to be cooperative. Instead, say, "I like you. But I DO NOT want to have sex with you." If he does not respond, say, "If you continue, I will consider this rape" and "I want you to stop now!" By being clear, you know that you expressed yourself directly, and so does he. Leave him no freedom to misunderstand your feelings.

Conclusion: Who Is Your Knight in Shining Armor?
YOU ARE! Now you have some strategies to recognize, avoid, and better handle an attack. The foundation of your self-defense is your self-confidence. If there is one thing I want you to learn, it is that you have the capacity to defend yourself. It may be frightening, but you can do it. If you can protect yourself in this most basic way, I believe you can do anything. You can depend on your own body and mind to be your knight in shining armor.

3

PHYSICAL SELF-DEFENSE SKILLS

In the last chapter we discussed verbal self-defense, body language, and the psychology of the attacker as keys to understanding the dynamics of an attack. In this chapter, we are going to add to your self-defense arsenal some physical self-defense techniques and strategies. For many women, learning self-defense can be difficult, but the difficulty has nothing to do with coordination, athletic ability, or physical strength. Instead, women feel intimidated about learning self-defense, because many lack confidence in their ability to protect themselves. Of course, it is necessary to know self-defense techniques, but they will be ineffective if you do not have the confidence to use them. When used together, awareness, confidence, and physical strategies are the fundamental elements of successful self-defense.

Before we continue with the specifics of physical self-defense, there are some general concepts you should keep in mind when reading this chapter. The most important is "committing yourself to the fight." As I have said before, defending yourself in any way is about making decisions. When you decide to use physical self-defense, you have to mentally commit yourself to the fight. What this means will be different for every woman, but primarily your commitment is based on the confidence that you can fight back. The most devastating disadvantage you can have in a fight is to have no faith in your ability. I believe that if someone attempts to physically hurt me, I am committed to fighting back until he leaves or is incapacitated. If he is threatening my life, I will fight until I literally die from trying. However, you do not have to share my view. Take a moment now and ask yourself, "Am I willing to fight?" And if you are, at what point are you willing to do so? When wouldn't you be, and why? What are some other possible solutions for you? Whatever your answer to these questions, know where you stand. If you are ever in a situation where physical self-defense is an option, reaffirm this commitment. Listen to your inner voice. Your strength will carry you through.

It is helpful to practice the techniques you will learn in this book. For this reason, women's self-defense programs are discussed in detail in the end of the chapter.

The other concepts are more specific:

Your muscles should be as relaxed as possible. I know some of you are saying right now, "How I am supposed to be relaxed during an attack?" It is very difficult to relax in any stage of an attack. But you need to try, because the more relaxed your muscles are, the more power you will have. If you are tense and simultaneously try to hit the attacker, your muscles will be using precious energy to maintain their tension instead of working to focus power into your technique.

All techniques taught in this chapter are simple and have a wide margin of error. You don't have to worry about which hand corresponds to which leg. When I explain a technique, I will tell you what stances are optimal, but in a real self-defense situation you should never worry about which hand or leg is striking. There are two different types of techniques:

distraction and destruction. A distraction technique will force the attacker to focus attention on himself, which enables you to follow up with a more destructive technique.

Whenever possible, you want to keep an attack from becoming physical. The techniques taught in this chapter are to be used when someone verbally and/or physically threatens you. If a man leers at you or says something offensive but does not get into your physical space, walk away. Our world is too dangerous to incite a confrontation.

Basic Techniques

One of the most difficult aspects of physical self-defense is knowing when to make the transition from verbal self-defense to physical self-defense. You need to understand when it is appropriate to fight back and when it is not, because you want to avoid a physical confrontation if at all possible. For example, imagine it is night and you are alone on the street. A man who appears homeless approaches you and asks for money. You avoid him, but he continues to follow you. You might easily be torn by a number of feelings: fear, because you are isolated; anger, because this person is invading your space; and empathy, because he is homeless. What is the most fitting response? If you do not feel that he is verbally and/or physically threatening you, it is inappropriate to use physical self-defense. If you want him to leave you alone, verbal self-defense will probably work. But if he grabs you or says something that indicates he intends to, physical self-defense is a justifiable course of action.

Use physical self-defense as your last resource, because most attacks can be stopped using verbal self-defense, and, in a fight, you could lose. Violence of any kind is serious, and the outcome unpredictable. Defending yourself physically, whatever the result, will most likely have a profound effect on your life. Understand that you are capable of inflicting considerable pain and injury to another person. To responsibly and effectively learn self-defense, you must respect your ability to defend yourself and the attacker's ability to hurt you.

All the physical self-defense skills presented in this chapter are applicable in any situation. Whether you are dealing with a stranger, an acquaintance, or a date, the techniques are the same. Your responsibility is to match the individual situation with an appropriate response. That said, physically hurting someone can be very difficult to think about, let alone to actually do, because women are raised to nurture, to be kind and loving. Very few women are raised to feel comfortable expressing anger. It is common in our classes for a woman to apologize after she has hit the male instructor during a simulated attack. Using physical self-defense is learning how to channel fear into anger and anger into action. Most of my students have never hit someone and cannot imagine doing it.

Before taking this course I had never hit anyone, never fought physically with anyone. The first day [of class] I was not sure I could fight back, because I could not imagine doing it. But I quickly overcame that fear. Before, if I felt myself in some danger, I would look for places to run or hope that nothing would happen. Now I try to anticipate what could possibly happen and what I can do to defend myself.

Violence against women makes me very angry. Learning self-defense is important because we understand that it's okay to be angry and we learn how to deal with unprovoked attacks without always being afraid of men.

The thought of hurting someone is a frightening one . . . I think it may be hard to hit someone, because I have always been taught not to. However, in the scenarios [in class], I felt a powerful sense of violation . . . and that made me angry.

If you don't think you could ever hit someone or you cannot imagine doing the things I suggest, don't worry. It is natural to feel this way. Temporarily push these thoughts out of your mind when you read this chapter. If you can do that, you will absorb more information. Then, if you should ever need to use physical self-defense, you may be able to recall the information more effectively. As one sixteen-year-old high school student remarked: "Before taking this course, I felt that violence against women was wrong but often inevitable. Now I feel that it is completely unacceptable and should not be tolerated in any form."

Here are the fundamental techniques for effective self-defense. Each description is followed by an illustration that demonstrates how the technique is applied.

FIGHTING STANCE

The fighting stance is the way you stand when you feel threatened. Have your hands up, elbows down, and knees slightly bent, and keep your feet about shoulder width apart. For extra stability, place one foot in front of the other (Fig. 1).

Fig. 1. Fighting stance   **Fig. 2. Relaxed fighting stance**

If you are in a situation where you feel uncomfortable and are unsure of the person's intentions, have your hands up in a casual way. This second stance is just as effective as the first, because your hands are prepared but the body language is less confrontational (Fig. 2).

The fighting stance serves two purposes: one offensive and one defensive. In the last chapter I mentioned how important it is to create a safe distance between you and the attacker. With your hands up in the fighting stance, you are minimizing the distance your hands need to travel to effectively strike the attacker. Simultaneously you are prepared for any strikes coming toward you, because your arms and hands are in position to protect your torso and head. Be careful to keep your elbows down. By keeping your elbows down, you can better protect your torso from being hit.

HAND STRIKES

With all the hand strikes, your stance and your body's motion are the same, because you always want to use as much of your body's power as possible. Women are five times stronger in their lower body than in their upper body, so we want to use the lower body strength whenever possible. When you strike with your hands, use your lower body strength. Start the motion by pivoting on the ball of your back foot. This will move your hips into the strike. Basically your hand is like the tip of a cracking whip. But remember, the whip won't crack—and your strikes won't have force—unless you generate power from your feet and hips, which act as the base of the whip.

Eye Jab The eye jab is a distraction technique. It will probably not end a fight, but it will distract the attacker. To jab an eye, take one hand and place your fingers together and

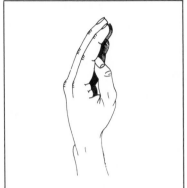

Fig. 3. Hand position for eye jab   Fig. 4. Eye-jab strike from
fighting stance

thumb underneath. Both fingers and thumb should be slightly
bent. You are striking with your fingertips. If you want to
understand how this technique feels, hit your striking hand
with medium strength into the palm of your other hand.
Now imagine that same force hitting your eye. The eye jab
does not have to be hard, but it does have to be accurate. It
accomplishes two things simultaneously: it prompts the attacker to take his hands off you, and it impairs his vision by
reducing his depth perception. (Figs. 3 and 4)

Palm Strike   While the eye jab is only effective to the eye,
the palm strike has numerous targets, incredible power, and
a wide margin of error. The basic difference between the
palm strike and the eye jab is the hand position. The primary
target is the nose but you can hit the mouth, chin, throat, or
ear. Begin in your fighting stance. You are hitting with the
palm of your hand, with your fingers pulled slightly back
(this is to avoid injury to your fingers during impact). Essentially the palm strike is a safe way to punch. It has the same
power as a punch but minimizes the risk of breaking your

hands or fingers. If you are short or your attacker is tall, a palm strike to the throat or Adam's apple is very effective. (Figs. 5 and 6)

There are two things to remember with hand strikes. You must strike quickly and return quickly. Think of your hands as weapons that, once they shoot out, must return immediately. Bringing your hands back is just as important as striking quickly, because you want to avoid letting your arms be used against you. If you leave them extended, the attacker can swat them out of the way or grab them. (But don't worry, the fight is not over if he does; keep reading.)

You also want to avoid telegraphing. Telegraphing means showing the attacker what you are going to do before you do it. You want the attacker to realize he has been hit when he feels it, not when he sees your hands preparing to strike. The element of surprise is critically important in women's self-defense. Especially with the first strike, do not let him know what is coming. With the hand strike this means two things: do not have your hand placed in the eye-jab position as soon as you're in the fighting stance, and do not pull back one of your

Fig. 5. Hand position for palm strike

Fig. 6. Palm-strike application

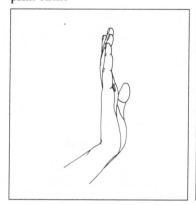

shoulders before you strike. Hand strikes begin straight out of your fighting stance and return to the same position.

Remember that with both hand strikes, you can increase your strength by two methods. First, pivot on your back foot as you are striking with your hand. You are pushing off on the ball of your back foot so that your leg and hip can generate power into the hand. Second, relax. If you are tense, most of your energy is going to be spent maintaining the tension. If you can relax, your muscles will have more freedom to move.

These techniques really work. Margaret, an adult graduate of our course, was attacked outside her home when she was returning from work. She was trying to get through her door when the assailant attempted to hit her. She moved out of the way and responded with an eye jab. It did not land in his eye, because he turned his head to the side to avoid it. But by turning his head, he exposed his ear and neck. She followed up with a palm strike, with her hand cupped, to his ear. He fell to the ground, and she continued with a kick to his face. She rushed into her house, locked all the doors, and called the police.

FRONT KICK

All strikes with the legs are done with the rear leg, because you can cover a greater distance and maintain your strength and stability. Begin in your fighting stance and lift your rear knee forward. From there, extend your leg and foot forward. Do not strike with your toes, because you will injure them and such a strike demands greater accuracy. Instead, strike with the top of your foot, the instep. When you retract the kick, reverse these motions; bend the knee and move the leg behind you. Placing your leg behind you increases your stability and power. (Figs. 7a–d)

Visualize what we are doing in combination and all this will become clear:

Fig. 7a. Starting position for
front kick (fighting stance)

Fig. 7b. Fold for front kick

Fig. 7c. Extension of front kick

Fig. 7d. Retraction of front kick
(fighting stance)

1. You jab his eye—he covers his eye.
2. You palm strike the nose—his body opens to you.
3. You front-kick him in the groin—he falls forward.

If you have your kicking leg firmly behind you, you will
remain stable even if he falls toward you. All you have to do
is sink your weight on your back foot. However, if you use

your front foot, you will have nothing with which to stabilize yourself, and you may fall with him. (If this happens don't panic. There are ways to deal with this. Keep reading.)

The front kick's primary target is the attacker's groin. Kicking into the general pelvic area is not sufficient. You must kick between the attacker's legs and then up. You want to directly ram the testicles up against the body. This is a kick that disables the attacker.

Because the kick to the groin can be a fight-ending strike, most men grow up instinctively knowing how to protect their genitals. The first thing an attacker will protect is his groin. Do not be discouraged. Whenever one target closes, another one opens. If he blocks his groin, he will have to bring his legs together and/or turn to the side. No problem. Now, what targets are available to you? His shins, thighs, and knees. Front-kicking to any of these areas is an excellent distraction technique. None will end a fight, but it will give you the opportunity to follow up with a more damaging strike.

The "one target opens when another closes" concept applies to all physical self-defense. Earlier I mentioned an attacker grabbing an arm or leg during a fight. If this happens, don't give up. When he grabs something of yours, he will expose another target. For example, if you kick to the groin and he grabs your kicking leg, what can you do? First, grab onto him for stability (use him as a leg). By grabbing your leg, he must lower his arms, thereby exposing his face to a strike. Your choice in this situation is to strike with either an eye jab or a palm strike. Suppose you choose a palm strike. And he responds by pulling his hands up to block. Now what's open? His groin. Always look for open targets, and take advantage of their vulnerability. If you can respond to a situation with this kind of flexibility, you have mastered one of the most important skills of self-defense.

I mentioned before that there is no way to predict how an

assault will occur or what your surroundings will be, and these are both critical factors in a fight. A graduate of our program was walking to her car and saw a man approaching her who made her feel uncomfortable. Trusting her instincts, she opened her car door and tried to get in, but he rushed toward her and pushed her into the car. The car had two doors, and she had left the seat back resting against the steering wheel. She was pushed face down, sandwiched between the seat and the seat back, and he began attacking her from behind. She tried to get up, but each time he would hit her head from above. She quickly realized her strategy would not work, so she thought about what she had to use against him. She knew he could not move freely without releasing her. She planted her feet on the road and used her legs and back to suddenly and powerfully straighten the seat back. She straightened it so quickly that she smashed the back of his head against the top of the door frame and ran to safety.

ROUND KICK

While the front kick allows you to strike in a straight line, the round kick is used to strike the side of the body. The motion of this kick is circular. It travels in an arc from your back foot to the target. From your fighting stance, the leg in back is the kicking leg and the front leg is the pivoting leg. Pivot on the ball of your front foot while raising the knee of your back leg. Continue pivoting and raising your knee until it is pointing straight at your target and your supporting foot is pointed in the opposite direction. Extend your kicking leg, and strike with your instep. Your target areas are the back and side of the knee, the thigh, and the back of the leg. There is never any reason to kick higher than your attacker's waist. If you kick higher you expose your groin as a target, and by kicking lower you preserve your stability. (Figs. 8a–d)

Fig. 8a. Starting position for round kick (fighting stance)

Fig. 8b. Fold for round kick

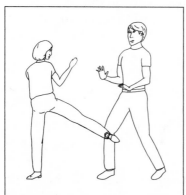

Fig. 8c. Extension of round kick

Fig. 8d. Retraction of round kick (fighting stance)

KNEES

There are two primary targets with the knee: the attacker's groin and his head. You start exactly the same way as with the kick, but you don't extend the foot. When you knee to the groin, pull the attacker into you. This may seem contrary to reason, but you want to pull the attacker into you because

Fig. 9. Knee strike to groin   Fig. 10. Knee strike to head

a knee to the groin is effective only if you can close the distance between you. At the same time as you are pulling in, you also want to pull your body toward his side. Pulling to the side minimizes his ability to hit you and avoids smashing your face into his. (Fig. 9)

Kneeing to the head is another fight-ending strike. You can only attempt this strike when his body is partially bent over—for example, after he has been kicked in the groin. In almost every situation you cannot push the attacker down toward the ground, because he will most likely be stronger than you. To perform this maneuver, place your hands on the attacker's head. But do not do this by grabbing his hair with your fists—he could reach around, hit your hands, and break your fingers. Instead, open your hands and hold the head like a ball. You will have the best control if you can cup one of your hands behind his neck. Now bring up the back leg and knee to the head. The higher the knee the better. It doesn't matter what part of your knee strikes as long as it's solid. When you practice, make sure that your knee is going through your hands. If your arms are fully extended, your knee will probably not go through your hands. (Fig. 10)

Here are the steps in combination (Figs. 11a–e).

Fig. 11a. Eye jab

Fig. 11b. Palm strike

Fig. 11c. Front kick to groin

Fig. 11d. Reaching to grab
assailant's clothes or neck

Fig. 11e. Knee to target

THIS SEQUENCE ILLUSTRATES AN
EFFECTIVE WAY TO PRACTICE
THESE TECHNIQUES IN
COMBINATION

ATTACKS FROM BEHIND

If you are attacked from behind or from the side, you need to immediately break the attacker's hold on you and create space between the two of you. In this situation, you can't use your arms against his hold effectively, because you have to rely on your physical strength. Instead, when you are touched, immediately yell and round your shoulders. This is done most easily by crossing the wrists. You are doing this because rounding your shoulders protects your sternum and lungs if you are forcibly grabbed from behind. To test the importance of rounding your shoulders, have a friend put his/her arms around you and squeeze. You should feel considerable pressure. Now round your shoulders and have the person squeeze you again. You should feel no discomfort. (Fig. 12a)

Next, look for the attacker's closest foot, and stomp on it. The easiest and most effective way is to stomp with your foot perpendicular to the attacker's, not parallel. You want to stomp *across* his foot. The foot stomp is one of my favorite techniques because it's easy and effective, and if you can break

Fig. 12a. Crossing wrists and
rounding shoulders

Fig. 12b–c. Foot stomp

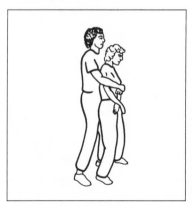
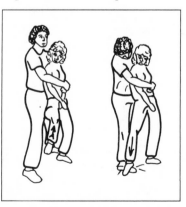

a bone in the foot, you make it considerably more difficult for an attacker to run after you. (Figs. 12b–c)

If you stomp with your right foot, your subsequent techniques will also use the right side. The next step is a hammer strike to the groin. A hammer strike is when you make a fist and swing your arm as you would a hammer. The hammer strike is not necessary if the foot stomp has loosened or broken the attacker's hold. The important thing is to break his hold. (Figs. 12d–e)

The hammer strike is followed by an elbow to the attacker's face. The elbow can deliver a devastating, fight-ending strike. To begin, look at your target (the attacker's face or throat), and raise your arm to your face level. Next, and in one motion, bend your arm so that your elbow protrudes, and strike behind you. Place all your weight into the strike, so your whole body is behind the elbow, not just the muscles in your arms. For example, if I am striking with my right elbow, I move my right arm across my body, bending it at the elbow, and then move it back to the right to strike. At the same time, my right foot takes a step closer to the attacker, so I will be able

Fig. 12d. Preparation for hammer strike

Fig. 12e. Hammer strike

Fig. 12f. Preparation for elbow strike

Fig. 12g. Elbow strike

to transfer my weight into the strike. The elbow strike should bring your body around so that you are facing the attacker. Once you are facing the attacker, you can follow up with the techniques you already know: the eye jab, the palm strike, the front kick, etc. (Figs. 12f–g)

About nine months after graduating from a Woman's Way basic course, a high school graduate was attacked from behind while she was walking through the automatic door of her neighborhood grocery store. The attacker, who was either drunk or on drugs, grabbed her around the waist and was attempting to pull her away, when she elbowed him in the sternum so hard that he fell to the ground. As he lay on the ground, she screamed at him that he shouldn't attack women, and then she went into the store. What I especially like about this success story was that she didn't stick to the combination procedures but chose instead (because her hands were free) the technique that would cause the greatest destruction in the shortest time.

FALLING

One of the most common ways women are injured during an attack is when they are thrown or pulled to the ground. Approximately 80 percent of the women assaulted each year are on the ground at some point during the attack. Think about what you do when you slip or trip. The most natural reaction is to break a fall with your hands and/or elbows. In falling backwards, someone who does not know how to fall well will allow her back to absorb most of the impact and will then hit the back of her head. Both can cause serious injury. This is also the time when it is possible to have the wind knocked out of you—so that immediately after a fall you panic and are unable to breathe. Now think about how dangerous it is when a woman falls or is thrown during an attack—the fight can be over at that moment. But it doesn't have to be.

Falling Forward   No matter what, falling face forward will be unpleasant. It's a matter of degree. The best way to fall forward incorporates three elements. As you fall, turn your face to the side, extend your forearms in front of your chest (palms facing out), and exhale as you hit the ground. Some of my students came up with the idea of crossing their arms in front of their chests as they fall. They say it hurts less. By falling like this, you avoid hitting your face on the ground. Falling forward will sting your breasts and forearms, but it will not incapacitate you. (Figs. 13a–d)

Falling Backwards   This fall applies when you are pushed or if you fall backwards. Visualize rolling backwards, not falling. To practice, begin by kneeling on one knee, and roll back by collapsing your torso. You want to roll off your spinal column, shoulders rounded and chin tucked into your neck.

Fig. 13a. Walking

Fig. 13b. As you fall, extend
forearms and turn face
to the side

Fig. 13c. As you hit the ground,
exhale and allow your forearms to
absorb the impact of the fall

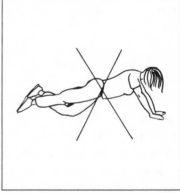

Fig. 13d. The wrong way to fall

From a standing position the same concepts apply. However, as you are standing, you have to be careful that your knee does not smash into the ground as you fall. From your fighting stance, begin by placing your weight on the front

leg. The next step is to collapse your back leg and to fall
back, so that the outside of your leg and knee takes the brunt
of the fall. As you fall, keep your chin tucked into your neck,
breathe out, and round your shoulders. (Figs. 14a–d)

If you are saying to yourself, "I could never remember to
do all these things," try to remember the most critical elements. Tuck your chin into your neck, round your shoulders,

Fig. 14a. Weight transfer

Fig. 14b. Collapse back leg

Fig. 14c. Roll backwards,
chin tucked and exhaling

Fig. 14d. Hitting the ground

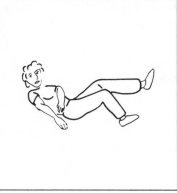

and exhale by yelling the moment before impact. If you can do any of these steps, you will be better off.

GROUND FIGHTING

Most women feel that they are totally helpless on the ground, because they imagine the attacker towering over them. In fact, there is no reason to be helpless on the ground. Most of my students, once they learn ground-fighting strategies, prefer to fight on the ground because their techniques are so much stronger. I emphasize ground fighting in women's self-defense for two reasons: 80 percent of women end up on the ground during an attack; and women are better fighters on the ground because on average they are five times stronger in their legs than in their upper body.

Just as you have a fighting stance when you are standing, you also have a fighting stance on the ground. It is called the kicking position. Lie on your side, and place one leg up in the air and parallel to the ground with your foot pointing straight up. The other leg is bent with the foot as close to the body as possible and should be completely touching the ground. Propped up on one elbow, place both hands on the same side as the leg touching the ground. It is very important to maintain stability and protect your torso and head while in the ground-fighting stance. If you keep both hands on one side, you will do both. (Fig. 15)

Your top leg is your weapon. When it is not striking, it should be held as close to your body as possible—try to pull your knee to your shoulder. The leg on the bottom should be resting on the ground for stability. A good kicking position should make you feel stable and protected. If you fall to the ground during a fight, stay down and immediately get into your kicking position. (Fig. 15)

IN A SELF-DEFENSE SITUATION,
ASSUME A KICKING POSITION
AFTER FALLING

Fig. 15. Kicking position

FRONT KICK

From your kicking position, extend the top leg directly toward your target. Be careful that your leg is moving directly forward with minimal wasted motion. You are kicking with your heel. If the attacker is on the ground, your primary targets are the head, groin, and knees. If he is standing and you are on the ground, strike the knees and the groin. The front kick is also good for pushing the attacker away from you—if, for example, the attacker has grabbed your kicking leg. Do not panic. Switch legs so that the leg on the ground is now the kicking leg and vice versa. (Figs. 16a-b)

If it is impossible to keep the leg on the ground because he is holding it, relax the leg and use him for stability. Then use your free leg to kick. In this situation, I recommend an ax kick (see next paragraph), because in order to grab you he must be very close to you and will therefore be vulnerable to this fight-ending kick.

 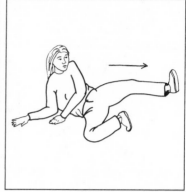

Fig. 16a. Starting position (kicking position)   **Fig. 16b. Extension of front kick**

FRONT KICK FROM THE GROUND

AX KICK

The ax kick is a devastating strike. One ax kick can knock someone out. The ax kick is used almost exclusively when the attacker is on the ground. To do the ax kick, begin in your kicking position. Then take your top leg and straighten it so that it is perpendicular to the ground. The higher you can get your leg up the better. Extending with the heel, bring your leg down onto the target area. Your primary target areas are the head and groin, but this kick is so powerful that you can kick the attacker anywhere and it will hurt. Be careful to bend your leg on impact, or you may hyperextend your knee. (Figs. 17a–b)

BEING PINNED

For many women, being pinned is the most frightening situation they can imagine, because they feel helpless. While we teach a specific self-defense technique against the pin in our class, you don't have to know it to get out of a pin. Especially

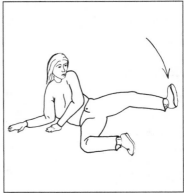

Fig. 17a. Fold for ax kick   Fig. 17b. Extension of ax kick

AX KICK ON THE GROUND

in this situation, cooperative verbal self-defense is critical. The reason a pin is so dangerous is that the attacker can easily hit you. You need to assure the attacker immediately that he is in control and you will cooperate. In a pin you have to lull the attacker into believing you will not resist.

Of course, I do not want you to really give up. Cooperating with him is only a strategy. He must first feel that you are under his control so that he can proceed with the sexual assault. Within that period is a window of opportunity for you to exploit. There is a moment when you have a chance. Specifically, he must take off some of his clothes and some of yours, or he will tell you to do it. So while you are saying, "Okay, I'll do whatever you want," or you are volunteering to take your clothes off (so that he lets go of you), strategize. Where are you going to hit him? When? In this situation I almost always recommend an eye jab followed by another destructive technique. You should end the fight with ax kicks to the head and groin. When he has stopped moving, get up and away from him, and run to safety.

If he wants to rape you from behind, you will be in a position in which you can easily turn around. To practice, get on your hands and knees, slightly push up on your toes so that your knees clear the ground, and drop into your kicking position. When you land, you will almost always be in a good position to strike with a front kick to the attacker's groin. (Figs. 18a–c)

These are the basic techniques of physical self-defense. Practicing them is essential, because if a real situation demands that you use physical self-defense, you will want your body to respond automatically. As there are infinite variables

Fig. 18a. Preparation for reversal

Fig. 18b. Rotating hips into kicking position

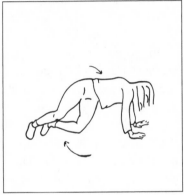

Fig. 18c. Kicking position

REVERSAL FROM REAR ATTACK ON THE GROUND

that can affect the outcome of a fight, the most important thing to remember is that these techniques work in any combination. Look for vulnerable targets to strike, and never give up.

Practicing

If you want to practice, here are some safe and inexpensive suggestions. One of the golden rules is: DO NOT PRACTICE ON FAMILY MEMBERS, FRIENDS, OR SIGNIFICANT OTHERS, UNLESS YOU USE EXTREME CAUTION! I guarantee that if someone you know sees you practicing these techniques and he is male, he will probably say something like, "Okay, well, what would you do if I did this?", and then he will seize your hands or legs. Although it can be tempting, do not demonstrate on him, because you could cause serious injury. It's also an unfair situation because he will grab you as hard as he can, but you can't hit him as hard as is necessary to prove the technique works. If you want to practice with someone, be very careful, start slowly, and constantly check your distance so you do not accidentally hit your practice partner.

Many women do not believe in their own physical strength. Believe me, you are strong, and you need to respect this strength. A few years ago I had a nice, gentle seventeen-year-old in a high school class. One school day a male student was bothering her, and she said jokingly, "Stop it, or I am going to use my self-defense." He laughed. She hit him with a palm strike. When she told me about it, she was astonished; she swore she hit him very lightly. Nevertheless, the boy had to go to the hospital with the worst bloody nose the school nurse had ever seen. It was obviously not appropriate to use physical self-defense in that situation. However, this experience demonstrated to this woman and the other students that if she could hurt someone that badly, all of them could. From then on, they had greater respect for their own power.

PRACTICING HAND TECHNIQUES

Stand in front of a mirror, and slowly do an eye jab. Your striking point should be about five inches from the mirror's surface. To increase your accuracy, pick a place in the mirror that you can aim for each time. Do the same exercise for the palm strike. Be careful that your palm is extended forward and fingers are pulled back. Frequently check your distance to avoid damaging the mirror!

If you want to practice striking with impact, get three or four firm pillows and tape them together with duct tape. To practice front kicks, place the pillows against a strong wall, get into your kicking position, and kick the pillows. Remember to keep your leg moving directly forward, instead of floating up first and then moving forward. Remember to bring your kicking leg back quickly.

To practice ax kicks place the pillows on the ground about two to three feet away from you (depending on how long your legs are). Raise your leg, drop it down, extend your heel, and kick into the pillows. When you have completed the kick, return your kicking leg to its original position.

USING TECHNIQUES IN COMBINATION

These techniques work best when they are used in combination. As there are an infinite number of ways of being attacked, one specific combination will not work in every situation. Rather, look for openings on the attacker, and assess the weapons you have at your disposal. For example, if a man grabs both of your hands, you obviously cannot strike with your hands. In a fight, never fixate on the parts of your body that are of no use to you at that moment. If your hands are taken, don't spend time trying to free them. So what weapons do you have? Your legs. Go for a kick to the groin or the shins. If he then tries to grab your leg, he must let go of one of your hands. Then do a palm strike or an eye jab.

Once you decide to use physical self-defense, you must finish the fight so that he can't run after you. This means knocking the attacker out or causing complete incapacitation, unless he runs away himself. You may wonder, "Why can't I run away after I strike the attacker once?" There is a very important reason. Most men can outrun most women. For example, if you strike the attacker with an eye jab and do not follow up with another technique, he may have time to retaliate. Hurting the attacker a little can be worse than not hurting him at all. On the other hand, if the attacker turns and flees after one or two blows, that's great!

Choosing a Self-defense Program

In addition to reading this book, I strongly advise you to take a self-defense course. In the last decade women's self-defense programs have become an increasingly popular means for women to address their fears and gain a feeling of control in their lives. I know that all women, regardless of age, physical shape, or athletic ability, can learn to defend themselves. The only thing that holds women back from learning effective self-defense is a program that does not emphasize women's unique physical strengths and does not respectfully recognize their emotional reaction to violence. The following is a guideline for choosing a good self-defense program. And I do encourage you to take one, because there is no substitute for practicing in real life.

Start by watching a class. Talk to students who are taking the class or who have already completed the program. As with any business transaction, you need recommendations before you can make a good decision. In our program, I suggest that prospective students contact graduates of the program. If you do not know any students from the program, ask the instructor to help you contact some.

Which program you choose should greatly depend on your first impressions of the instructor. Watch him or her teach the class. Do not be intimidated by the martial-arts mystique. If he or she is condescending or arrogant, do not enroll in the program. Male instructors must understand that what works well for their bodies may be totally inappropriate for women's bodies. Ask them if they specifically gear their program to reflect how women's bodies work most effectively. If the instructor is female, be careful that she is not man-hating and does not emphasize women's victimization instead of women's strengths. A good instructor will respect what you have to say and focus on women's strengths.

Most women who want to learn self-defense are not doing so to dedicate their lives to a martial art. If you are interested in a program that is taught within a martial-arts school, be sure that is not taught as a part of the regular class curriculum. As women's self-defense has grown in popularity, many martial-arts schools advertise women's self-defense as a ruse to enroll women in their regular class. Good schools realize that women's self-defense and martial arts are separate pursuits.

Effective programs will teach simple techniques that have a wide margin of error. If you do not think you have the knowledge to ascertain the complexity of the program curriculum, ask the instructor if the techniques are easy to learn and have a wide margin of error. Specifically, stay away from programs that teach sweeps and joint locks. Sweeps are techniques where a person's balance is thrown off by having his legs literally swept from underneath him. Joint locks are complex techniques where a person's joints are forced into extremely painful positions. These types of techniques do not work on the street, unless you have years of training. Look for techniques that incorporate women's legs and hips; an instructor who teaches such techniques knows women's strengths.

As far as class size and duration, there really is no fixed rule. I think it is much more important that the program have a strong, positive philosophy. However, I find it difficult to teach groups larger than twenty. It's best to start with a short, less rigorous class and see if you like the program. Many schools offer different types of programs, which range in duration and intensity. That way you can take a class without making a huge commitment.

The best programs use a padded instructor to simulate physical assaults. These programs are the only ones that allow the students to fight back as hard as they can in a safe, controlled environment. It is not good enough to practice against targets and punching bags; neither can move or fight back as an attacker does. Equally important is that you have practice dealing with your emotional response to the physical confrontation. Most women do not have experience hitting someone as hard as they can. During the class, you realize how hard you need to hit someone and how your techniques affect the human body. As I said in the beginning of the chapter, women's self-defense is about having the confidence to fight back and responding appropriately to different situations.

I believe it is crucial that the head instructor in a women's self-defense program be a woman. Male instructors reinforce the stereotype that men are the only experts in self-defense. A woman instructor is visible proof that women are capable of self-defense. She is also more able to empathize with women's apprehension, and she is proof that fears can be overcome.

It is essential that there be frequent opportunities to discuss students' emotional reaction to the class and that the course be oriented toward women's empowerment; not toward man hating. Women's self-defense is more than teaching women how to protect themselves on the street. I believe a good program can fundamentally change a woman's perspective about her physical, mental, and emotional power.

4

THE DATE-RAPE DEBATE: FACT OR FICTION?

I am my choices.
Sartre

How do you define rape? What is date rape? Is it different from rape? Is verbal coercion rape? Can a man rape without intending to do so?

Whatever your answers to these questions, you have probably heard passionate arguments concerning them. While some people may dismiss date rape as a trendy media topic, I believe the issue demands closer examination. The way in which we discuss what is and what is not rape affects our ability to understand conflicting viewpoints in gender politics. All discussion at the moment seems to reflect a battle between an extreme part of the feminist movement, which does not represent all feminists, and a growing backlash in response to its apparent intolerance. Both are threatening the chance for effective and genuine dialogue, because their polarized political positions inhibit the free interchange of ideas in a respectful environment. We will never reach a middle ground on the dynamics and causes of rape if we do not commit ourselves to an open dialogue. We need to listen to both sides and encourage individuals to form their own opinions after careful consideration. At the present moment, our focus on reducing sexual violence has been diverted by the political agendas of the extremists and their opponents.

Before I go any further, I want to clearly explain what I mean by the extreme part of the feminist movement, because I myself am a feminist. I believe that the feminist movement seeks to address important issues concerning prejudice and bigotry, and the movement has succeeded in bringing to the national consciousness issues that have been traditionally hidden or unquestioned. I have also been incredibly fortunate in having strong women mentors to guide and educate me. But I believe there is an extreme, yet small and influential group within this movement that is significantly contributing to the way in which young men and women are miseducated about "appropriate" sexual behavior and interaction. For example, the recent college and university rules that demand consent for each sexual interaction (Antioch University's being the most famous) are absurd. Sex cannot be completely controlled by social rules. Guided, maybe. Controlled, absolutely not. And what are the results of this education?

I believe that the consequences of the current dialogue for young men and women are significant and detrimental; rigid opinions inhibit each sex from listening to and valuing the other's perspective and life experience. Moreover, extremists encourage young women to abdicate responsibility for the consequences of their own conduct, nurture a cultural expansion of the definition of rape to include behavior that is clearly not rape, and create an environment where people who disagree with some of the more overreaching definitions of rape feel uncomfortable voicing their dissent and challenging the "correct" status quo. The extreme-feminist message sets up women for blindly walking into potentially dangerous situations or believing that they have been raped when in fact they have not. Because of the date-rape hysteria, more and more people are demonstrating an intolerance for rape cases that do not fit traditional stereotypes.

The Spur Posse case in California is an excellent example of this growing intolerance. Nine members of the Spur Posse gang were arrested in March 1993 for forcing girls as young as ten to have sex. The gang was having a competition to see which member could have the most sex. One point was awarded for each girl, and the winner claimed to have sixty sex points. Many parents and students believed that the arrests were unfair. In the words of one boy's father, "They are being prosecuted for doing only what comes naturally to them. The real villains are the girls of loose morals who are now crying rape." (None of these girls was older than fourteen.) Another father remarked, "Nothing my boy did was anything that any red-blooded American boy wouldn't do at his age . . . I am proud of those virile specimens." And from the mother of the gang leader, "Those girls are trash." The boys returned to school as heroes.

The fundamental disagreement in this debate stems from the differences in which rape and sexual violence are defined. Defenders of particular definitions fight for supremacy. Most women define rape within their own context of male dominance, intimidation, and violence. They have grown up in a society where the fear of sexual assault is a daily threat, where their confidence in avoiding or resisting an assault is low, and where it does not take an overwhelming degree of male intimidation or threat to force a woman to comply with sexual demands.

Because our legal system is based on a male perspective, it is only natural that the legal definition of rape would greatly differ from women's experience of rape. *Black's Law Dictionary* defines rape as the following:

The act of sexual intercourse committed by a man with a woman not his wife and without her consent, committed when the woman's resistance is overcome by force or fear, or under other prohibitive conditions. A male who has sexual intercourse with a female not his wife is guilty of rape if (a) he compels her to submit by force or by threat of imminent death, serious bodily injury, extreme pain or kidnapping, to be inflicted on anyone, or (b) he has substantially impaired her power to appraise or control her conduct by administering or employing without her knowledge drugs, intoxicants, or other means for the purpose of preventing resistance, or (c) the female is unconscious. (p. 1260)

When rape survivors take their cases to court, the way they define the nature of "threat," "fear," "imminent death," and "intimidation" is usually at odds with these legal definitions. When women try to utilize the law to fight their battles, they usually lose. However, there are some states that now recognize that women can be raped by their spouses.

In *Trauma and Recovery* (HarperCollins, 1992), Judith Lewis Herman contrasts women's experience of rape with the legal definition of rape:

Women quickly learn that rape is a crime only in theory; in practice the standard for what constitutes rape is set not at the level of women's experience of violation but just above the level of coercion acceptable to men. Traditional legal standards recognize a crime of rape only if the perpetrator uses extreme force, which far exceeds that usually needed to terrorize a woman, or if he attacks a woman who belongs to a category of restricted social access . . . The greater degree of social relationship, the wider the latitude of permitted coercion . . . Indeed an adversarial legal system is of necessity a hostile environment; it is organized as a battlefield in which the strategies of aggressive argument and psychological attack replace those of physical force . . . The legal system is designed to protect men from the superior power of the state but not to protect women or children from the superior power of men.

Women are justified in their anger and frustration when the law does not incorporate women's perspectives in defining rape or acknowledge the different "reality" of fear between the sexes. But until the law changes, women must understand that, regardless of the debate surrounding rape, the reality is that the legal system was not created to reflect a woman's perspective. For example, if you voluntarily drink alcohol or ingest drugs, become sexually intimate with a man, and then have nonconsensual sex without expressly and adamantly voicing rejection, the law does not recognize this action as rape—no matter how much you believe you have been raped.

It is natural that our political, cultural, and educational institutions incorporate the law's definition of rape. Somehow, in the midst of these radical differences in perspective and power, we must strive for a middle ground. As women, we cannot simply vent our frustrations and then cloister ourselves with others who agree with our definitions. We must confront the disparity between our perspectives and the political and legal institutions, and work within the system for genuine change. At the same time, we must assume responsibility for our actions. It is in this way that women can begin to defend themselves against rape and date rape, and advance the agenda of sexual equality.

I believe the extremists' position on rape and date rape threatens our ability to reach this consensus. The potential for date rape has existed since women have had the freedom to choose their sexual partners. I define date rape as occurring when a man and a woman are to some degree previously acquainted, there is a degree of trust between the two, and nonconsensual sex occurs as a result of one person (almost always the man) not respecting a clear verbal or physical message that indicates he is acting against the will of the other. But the extremists' definition of date rape has recently been expanded to include situations where two people previously acquainted have nonconsensual sex when the woman does not clearly communicate what she wants, resulting in a confused set of verbal and physical messages. In an interview with National Public Radio in the fall of 1993, Robin Morgan, a former editor of *Ms.* magazine, clearly represents this perspective:

> There are many non-physical ways a man can pressure a woman into sex . . . If given her druthers, she wouldn't have [sex], but something is making her . . . whether it is a mild fear of his sulk . . . she's so exhausted, she doesn't want a scene . . . or it's just easier because otherwise it will be a production. The bottom line is that it was not something she wanted to do . . . I would like to see our definitions of rape expanded to include that.

This statement implies that women are so weak that rape laws should protect them not only from men but also from their own inability to articulate what they want. The opposite extreme, voiced by Camille Paglia in *Sex, Art, and American Culture,* is even more offensive and denigrating:

> Everyone knows throughout the world that many of these working class relationships where women get beat up have hot sex . . . [And] if [rape] is a totally devastating psychological experience for a woman, then she doesn't have the proper attitude toward sex. It's this whole stupid feminist thing about how we are basically nurturing, benevolent people, and sex is a wonderful thing between two equals. With that kind of attitude, then of course rape is going to be a total violation of your entire life, because you have had a stupid, naïve, Mary Poppins view of life to begin with.

I believe we need a new definition to describe a sexual act that does not fall clearly within the traditional definitions of rape. One person, the "aggressor," unintentionally uses power over another in a sexual context where the unwilling partner does not clearly communicate what she wants and the result is nonconsensual sex. Another way of seeing the situation is that the aggressor's intention is to have sex, but it is not his intention to have sex nonconsensually. Let's call it unintentional nonconsensual sex.

There is a problem here: What is clear communication? To answer this, I have explained strategies women should use in these situations (see chapter 2), but the advice bears repeating. For your own safety, you must communicate what you want explicitly. If you want to have sex, say so. If not, say no just as clearly. It is not appropriate to say no and simultaneously continue sexual interaction. For example, saying no while kissing someone is a mixed message. In addition, how you speak is as important as what you say, and what you communicate with your body is just as important as what you say with words. Do not state what you want in a passive, whining, unassertive manner. If he continues behaving in a manner that makes you feel that sexual intercourse is a possibility and he has not listened to you thus far, say, "If we have sex, I will consider it rape." If he continues, it should be clear to both of you, and, it is hoped, to the police, that he raped you.

There is an issue concerning intent that I would like to address. In my experience with young women, there seems to be a growing consensus that a date-rape survivor should be unquestionably believed when she describes the intent of her sexual partner and says that rape occurred. To me, this is another facet of women abdicating responsibility. I have heard numerous stories from my students about friends of theirs who have been date-raped. About half the stories are strikingly similar: the woman goes to a party, drinks excessively, gets together with a man, and later has sex with him. When she wakes up the next morning, she realizes that she's had sex with someone she never would have chosen had she been sober. On reflection, the woman decides that she was set up, that the man's intention was to coerce her with alcohol and then to have sex with her. While there are men who do this, women in this situation are not forced to drink—they decide to drink. They are not forced into isolation with a man—they willingly go. In this situation, there is no way to prove, or even suggest, that the man commits premeditated rape.

Intent, definitions, and communication are central to the date-rape debate, because the environment in which date rape occurs often includes an element of trust between two individuals. They are with each other of their own volition, and could be sexually attracted to each other. Sex and sexuality are confusing to most people, no matter what their age. Therefore, it is not surprising that during a date either date rape or unintentional nonconsensual sex can occur, but the two acts, when presented side by side, may appear indistinguishable to an outside observer. More important, each individual involved may see the same interaction in a completely different way.

Here is how I differentiate between date rape and unintentional nonconsensual sex. If a woman tells her date that she does not want to have sex, there should be no way he can initiate intercourse without understanding that he is acting against her will and is committing rape. Date rape may also occur when the woman is incapacitated or unconscious because of excessive ingestion of alcohol or drugs and is therefore unable to indicate her wishes. In both examples, the woman has been raped by her date, and the man should be dealt with like any other rapist. However, if a woman willingly places herself in a situation where sex is a realistic consequence, if she does not indicate her opposition to having sex in a direct, straightforward manner, and if her partner is therefore unable to understand her desire not to have sex, I believe that this is not rape but unintentional nonconsensual sex. In this situation, the woman should take as much responsibility as the man. Certainly, the man's responsibility is to make sure he knows what the woman wants by listening carefully and respecting her wishes. However, the social contract between the sexes has not changed so quickly or dramatically that women can now abdicate responsibility for their own behavior while holding men strictly accountable for theirs. That does not mean a woman is to be blamed for an assault, but she does need to hold herself accountable for not communicating clearly, making decisions that place her at greater risk (like drinking excessively), or sending mixed messages.

The unfortunate consequence of unintentional nonconsensual sex during a date is that a woman who has experienced it often feels just as bad as a woman who has been raped by her date. Worse, in both situations she may even feel more powerless because she was hurt by someone she knew and liked. But feelings of regret, no matter how valid, should not change the definition of rape to include situations where consent is unclear. To make rape anything other than nonconsensual sex achieved by verbal or physical threat or the use of force destroys the power of the word. Let rape stand alone, so that when someone says s/he has been raped, we know exactly what is meant. My fear is that as the definition of rape expands, the effect of the word will diminish until it is powerless to communicate its original meaning.

Let me give you an example of a negative consequence of expanding the definition of rape. An eighteen-year-old high school senior told me after class that she had been date-raped. When she later told me the story in detail, it was clear that she had not been date-raped. In fact, sexual intercourse never occurred, because her heavily intoxicated date fell asleep while they were arguing about whether they were going to have sex. Yet she believed that she had been raped because she felt her date's intent was to rape. This is an extreme example, but it shows that young women are being conditioned to think that, for a rape to occur, a woman merely perceive the intention of rape. I believe this is only one of the manifold negative consequences of this type of extreme-feminist rape "education."

To reduce violence in their lives, women can begin by taking responsibility for their actions. That means, at the very least, standing up for yourself and speaking out when anyone treats you without dignity and respect. Taking responsibility also means telling a date in a straightforward way whether or not you are interested in having sex. I know that there are many women who, because of their socialization or past experiences, find it extremely difficult to be assertive. But I also believe that all women, regardless of their personal histories, face a difficult choice: accept their fate as victims, or change their destiny by demanding punishment for what is clearly criminal behavior and by acknowledging their own responsibility for unintentional yet negligent behavior on a date.

Women are usually smaller and physically weaker, so to survive they have to be smarter. Violence is an integral part of our world, and it frequently manifests itself by the strong attempting to exploit the weak. Women's fear of rape has restricted their independence and led them to believe that they must rely on the good will and protection of men to remain physically safe. Recently, women have won some degree of authority and power in society, but the physical difference between men and women still means that men are physically, emotionally, and mentally more capable of protecting themselves and others. Until society fully incorporates women's perspectives into its social, political, and legal institutions, women must bear the responsibility of ensuring their own physical safety.

When I speak with young women, I frequently hear, "No means no. A woman can say no however she wants, and if he doesn't listen to her it's rape." Of course no means no. But so what? Just because you have a right does not mean that it will be respected. Words can mean different things to different people, on the basis of perceived tone, personal histories, and the situation. While it is good that women recognize they have the right to say no whenever and however they want, it is equally important that women know it is only the first step in stopping a potential date/acquaintance rape. Because in some date-rape situations, you must be clear, forceful, and repetitious to effectively communicate that you don't want to have sex. And isn't stopping a rape the goal? Even the extreme-feminist position, which can glorify victimization, does not intend for a young woman to join the ranks of those who have been hurt and feel victimized because she believes she has experienced date rape.

Assuming responsibility for one's actions is a key element of the problem. Life is about making decisions, and some are bound to be better than others. With each choice one makes, there is a possible risk or danger. (However, I am not talking about women who "choose" prostitution or "choose" to be with an abusive partner. Their "choices" are based on limited options and the need to survive. I am referring only to women who are with men of their own volition and who make decisions that place them at greater risk of assault.) And a woman does have choices in a date-rape situation. She can decide to avoid isolating herself with her partner. She can resist drinking alcohol to the point where she is unable to think clearly. A woman who hasn't taken responsibility for her actions is essentially saying, "I was powerless to stop it. Nothing I could have done, no decision I could have made would have made a difference." The implication is that the man was the only one capable of clearly communicating what he wanted and that the woman was helpless in the face of his coercion. If the woman wants to make sense of what happened (as much as that is possible) or avoid the recurrence of a similar experience, she needs to understand her behavior within that context. You can say "No means no" until you are blue in the face. The question I ask myself and others is "What is going to reduce a woman's risk of rape?" Talking about rights does not give women skills and strategies for avoiding rape.

Men and Women Discuss the Issue

To reach a better understanding of people's perspectives, I conducted several focus groups. These groups were not organized according to strict scientific procedure. My attempt was to get a better understanding of what both men and women thought about rape, what types of men are perpetrators, whether there is a difference between rape and date rape, and what, if any, are a woman's responsibilities in such a situation. Group members differed in age, gender, race, sexual orientation, and political viewpoints. More than half of the groups were all women or all men. Each group was presented with these scenarios for discussion.

SCENARIO 1
Liz goes out to a bar one evening with some friends. As the night progresses, some of her friends leave, and she doesn't have a ride home. Eventually she finds a male friend of a friend to give her a ride. Liz knows she has had too much to drink and passes out in the car, but she wakes up when they pull up to her house. They walk inside and he tries to make a pass at her, which she rejects. A few minutes later, she sits on the couch and he joins her. He pushes her down,

and she passes out again. When she awakens a few moments later, he is on top of her and has vaginally penetrated her.

SCENARIO 2

Tina is a third-year university student. She has been interested in a guy, Steve, in her political science class. They often talk after class and have developed a good rapport. One Saturday night, Tina goes to a campus party at a dormitory and runs into Steve. They immediately begin talking. They drink, dance, and generally have a great time. He invites her upstairs to his room and she willingly goes; the night has been great so far, she doesn't want the evening to end, and she is physically attracted to him. Once in his room, they start making out on the couch. He then tries to move her to the bed. She is really enjoying everything so far, but she doesn't want to have sex with him. As he gently pulls her to the bed, she says in a whining voice, "Can't we wait? I really like you, but I'm not sure. Steve, no . . . Can't we wait?" He responds, "Why? We like each other and we're having a great time. Let's stop playing games and have a good time." Tina asks once more if they can wait and then stops saying anything. They have sex. Once they are done, she runs out of the room.

Responses to these scenarios generated conflicting and heated discussions. With only one exception, people believed that the woman in the first scenario was raped. That one exception believed that rape did not occur because "there was no mention that her clothes were removed." (This individual did not realize that one can have sexual intercourse without being naked.)

The second scenario generated controversy. However, not all the women believed Tina was raped, and not all the men believed she was not. What was most interesting was that everyone's initial opinions became increasingly confused as other people's viewpoints were voiced.

WHAT WOMEN THOUGHT

In the second scenario, most of the women interviewed believed Tina was raped. She had said no, and that was all they needed to determine that rape occurred. A few others held Tina responsible because she drank to the point where her decision-making abilities were impaired. The following conversation between women occurred in a coed group.

> "She should have known better than to drink like that. It is her fault."
> "Well, she should have been more forceful with him. It probably would have helped her situation."
> "Why should the burden fall on her to be assertive? Is it okay to rape her if she isn't assertive?"
> "No. But there's a fine line. You can be nice and polite and still convey your message."

This interchange represents the spectrum of answers. Tina should not take responsibility for the rape, but she should take responsibility for drinking excessively. If she had been more assertive, she would have probably stopped the rape from occurring. It's not okay for Steve to rape her just because she isn't assertive. But the reality is that Tina is more likely to be taken advantage of if she is unable to stand up for what she wants or if she drinks to the point where she cannot assert herself.

If Tina is encouraged by her peers to press charges, what would be the most likely outcome? Most assistant district attorneys I spoke with said they would not accept the case, because the issue of consent was unclear. One assistant district attorney said she would accept the case if, immediately following the incident, Tina had spoken to a friend or relative, was upset when she spoke to that person, and claimed to have been raped. If Tina waited to tell someone or continued with her daily activities the next day, this district attorney would reject the case because there would be no way to conclusively prove a rape occurred. The outcome of the case rests on his story versus hers. In the district attorney's words, "When there are two reasonable accounts of a story, you must find for the defendant." Tina would probably then think she had received no justice and that the system was against her, and she would join the growing ranks of young women who feel they have been raped by a man and the system. The experience would leave her angry and feeling powerless. It is hard to imagine a feminist movement actively educating young women in a way that makes Tina's case typical. But that is exactly what some extremists are doing.

And what about Steve? If Tina presses charges, the police will take him down to the police station for questioning, even if the case is likely to be dismissed. What harm will be done to him? Clearly he did not suffer as badly as Tina, but the experience will probably enrage him, especially after his "vindication." But how will it affect his future relations with women? He has now "learned" that women cannot be trusted and he can be arbitrarily accused of rape. He will probably share his experience with friends, putting further strain on gender relationships on campus. Later, when Steve, Tina, and their friends leave college, they will carry their viewpoints into their workplace and social life.

CONSEQUENCES OF THE DATE-RAPE CONTROVERSY
FOR WOMEN

The politics of date rape is having dangerous consequences for young women. The extremists perpetrate and sustain a cycle of victimization where women perceive themselves as being weak and helpless. They are asked to wear their victimization, or "survival stories," as a badge of honor. Worse, I believe this cycle encourages women to identify themselves only through and because of the bad/abusive experiences they have had. What kind of positive image can you have of yourself if you see yourself first and foremost as a victim of another's abuse? It is insulting to all women if any one of us is identified exclusively by limited definitions that celebrate our pain and suffering instead of our power and strength. Women are more than that. We all have rich lives with good and bad experiences. And it is not what has happened to us that makes us who we are. It is how we respond and grow as a result of each new experience and challenge.

In addition, the extremists do not hold women accountable for their actions. In essence, the accepted belief is that doing so would be blaming the victim. I don't agree. It is possible to accept responsibility for actions that placed you at a greater risk for rape, but it does not necessarily follow that you are to be blamed for the rape. If women do not hold themselves responsible for their own care, then they are buying into the belief that they really are weak and powerless.

I am most concerned about some young women (almost always recent college graduates) I have come into contact with who consider themselves feminists while simultaneously demonstrating an intolerance for other women's opinions. For example, my belief that it is reprehensible for university students to accuse someone of rape by posting names of "rapists" on public bathroom walls is perceived as traitorous to feminism. In one case, a woman I was speaking with about date rape was so offended by my opinions that she backed away from the table where we were sitting, crossed her arms, and refused to listen to me. I have had more than one experience where women have said I was betraying all women by having these opinions. It was as if I uttered some buzzwords that immediately branded me an enemy and an antifeminist. Insulating oneself from reality will not stop rape. These intolerant people will serve only to alienate others and place themselves at greater risk of being raped, because they don't deal with the problem pragmatically.

Doing research and interviewing people for this book, I have met many women who have agreed with me. They have told me numerous stories about having expressed their feelings and concerns, only to be silenced by other women. During one interview, Mary said to me:

> The feminist movement is not keeping up with the reality of today and it will not acknowledge that women, as well as men, can be cruel. When a woman is raped, it should be a given that she didn't deserve it. But don't patronize or manipulate her by saying, "Poor baby." She needs to hear what she can do to recover. There is no glory in being a victim. She needs strategies so that this rape does not destroy her.

In all the discussion about rape, we become desensitized to what we are actually talking about. Rape hurts. It is an excruciating physical, emotional, and psychological injury. Although rape survivors often benefit from discussion, they desperately need survival strategies. They certainly do not need extremists who perpetuate and glorify victimization.

WHY LISTEN TO MEN?

When Woman's Way first began, I basically believed that men's opinions were worthless. In the years since, I have learned that the contributions men can make to understanding rape are invaluable. When I first started teaching, I wanted the male instructors to be nothing but punching bags. I wanted women to be the central authority figures at all times. However, I quickly realized that this attitude created an environment where the students were motivated by their common anger, fear, and hatred of men. Of course it's healthy to express your feelings, but it's unhealthy for only hatred and anger to motivate your actions. Gradually, the way in which the program was conducted changed to more fully incorporate the male instructors. As soon as the male instructors became equal participants in the program and had more freedom to express their feelings and thoughts, the atmosphere of the class changed. Our students realized that their male instructors truly cared about them and respected their fears, while the men felt good about being trusted. As a result, the class mood changed from one based on fear and hate to one based on empowerment through the positive support of every person in the class.

The male instructors' insights and contributions continue to be important. While I recognize that women's voices have been historically silenced and must now be heard, I believe that it is also critically important to listen to what men are saying about rape. I admit that when we include everyone's voice there is a constant risk that the issue will be lost in the din. But what other choice do we have to truly solve a problem that involves men and women? We are dangerously close to a situation where people will be unable to express their thoughts or feelings for fear of not saying what is correct, or will be so alienated by rape politics that they will dismiss the problem entirely. The process of ending violence against women must be founded on an intergender dialogue based on a respect for and understanding of different perspectives.

Like the women, men in the focus groups differed from one another in their reactions. From the intensity of the discussions, this issue is clearly important to men and one about which they feel strongly. Sometimes you hear opinions that you thought existed only in the past.

If you willingly walk into a war zone, you have no one to blame but yourself if you step on a mine . . . Most of our laws are based on actions, because no one can get inside anyone's head. Rape used to rely on physical evidence, such as torn clothes or bruises. In these scenarios there probably would not have been anything like that. Even if there were, it could have been enthusiastic sex. Maybe she wanted it that way, but she's afraid to admit it so she sets up the situation [as a rape].

This man makes you realize how much more needs to be done in terms of rape awareness. It does not occur to him that if the woman had "enthusiastic sex" but was embarrassed about it, it would have been easier for her not to say anything about it in the first place.

But not all men saw the situation like that. In fact, this man was in the minority. Generally, the men did communicate two concepts clearly: (1) women must articulate what they want in a straightforward manner, so that there is no room for a man to misunderstand a woman; and (2) there are men who will take advantage of an unassertive woman.

If she can't openly discuss with the guy the specifics of what she wants, then she shouldn't be making out with the guy. If she can't say, "Listen, this is what I want," then she should know better than to get herself into a situation like that.

I hope that if I was in that situation I would stop. I think I would, but I can see how a guy could be confused. In the second scenario, she whines and asks, "Can't we wait?" That is not saying, "I don't want to have sex now." That is sending mixed signals, and she is putting the responsibility on him by asking him. When she does that, she is putting the decision to have sex in his hands. And he basically says, "No, we can't." Women need to be more assertive. Steve's actions are wrong, but if a woman is not assertive, there are men who will take advantage of that.

There were other men who believed that Steve was entirely at fault.

> It's not the woman's obligation to be assertive. I don't care if she is laughing and she says no. If she says no, I am going to ask her if she really wants to have sex. If she really means no. It's this type of case that makes rape so difficult to define. We need a legal definition of what date rape is, and there isn't one, and that's why we have all these questions.

> It doesn't matter how she says no, because if she says no, there should be no analyzing. Even if the guy thinks she means yes, it shouldn't matter, because she said no.

What are these men saying that can make women safer? In a date-rape situation, women must communicate clearly what they want, because some men won't stop trying to persuade a woman to have sex unless she forcibly says no. One man compared the situation to a puppy being told not to do something and not listening until it is swatted on the nose with a newspaper. What also came across is that most men think there are men who do try to take advantage of women. Women need to realize this, take precautions, and act decisively when faced with this type of individual.

THE CONSEQUENCE OF DATE RAPE FOR MEN

The radical politics of date rape has four detrimental consequences. First, it reinforces the stereotype that all feminists and the policies they support are radical and out of touch. The vast majority of men and women I speak with generalize that all feminists are radical; therefore, these men and women want nothing to do with the larger feminist movement. Second, men feel uncomfortable expressing opinions that make them appear chauvinistic. Third, men resent what they perceive as the feminist assumption of guilt until innocence is proven. And fourth, men now believe that they could have consensual sex, and then be accused and convicted of rape. Although the facts speak to the contrary—about one percent of all people accused of rape are convicted—we must understand and respect men's fears. Many of the men I have spoken with are very angry at the current political tide of date rape. They believe that they could be victims of an arbitrary accusation. Unfortunately, if this state of affairs continues, the polarization between men and women will make open-minded discussion impossible.

> The atmosphere in which these things are handled now has gotten so far out of control that an accusation is now a conviction. It's like a witch-hunt.

> There is a philosophy of victimization today. When something bad happens, somebody is always somebody's victim regardless of the facts of the case. I think this [philosophy of victimization] ties into the whole rape issue well, in that it's almost a Victorian scenario: weak-willed women are always pushed around by strong men. I think women are better than that.

> It seems that now everyone is trying to get a slice of the compensation pie. It's as though women are saying, "I'm a victim, too, and I'm more of a victim than you are." You are socially favored because you are a victim. It is very unpopular in America to take responsibility for your actions when you can blame someone else.

These men are reacting to the intolerance they feel from the extremists. If our goal is to increase communication between the sexes so that the definition and dynamics of date rape become clearer to everyone, the current dialogue is defeating the purpose. And if the extreme part of the feminist movement alienates people, its counterpart uses this alienation to justify dismissing women's fears and experience of rape.

CAN A MAN RAPE A WOMAN IF HE TRULY BELIEVES THAT HIS PARTNER IS CONSENTING TO SEXUAL INTERCOURSE?

This is a hard one. The men I spoke with voiced this concern with considerable apprehension. Even if a man was found not guilty, his peers might still assume he is guilty. One young man in a focus group consistently said there was no way he could imagine ever getting into a date-rape situation, because he would always be very clear with his partner. However, as the discussion progressed, he realized something very frightening:

> I never see this as a problem for me, because if there was any doubt I would stop. But I can see that I could have consensual sex with someone and she could later call it rape. There is a movement now, so many more people are aware of date rape. Because of that, maybe it is easier to accuse someone of rape, and he could be found guilty. And if you compare the story of a girl who actually was raped with a story of a girl who had consensual sex and later called it rape, the jury would hear the same thing. The stories would be the same, but one would be a rape and the other wouldn't. That's really scary.

This young man was a sensitive, caring person. During the discussion, he openly agreed with the women in the group who held Steve responsible for raping Tina. But he also realized how difficult it can be to distinguish a real date rape from a false one. If this young man is faced with a situation like Steve's, will he react by refusing to acknowledge his responsibility and will he only become desensitized and angry? We need to give him knowledge, so that he does not believe he is being punished for a crime he did not commit. Perhaps, in this way we can stop the cycle of misunderstanding, abuse, and anger.

The consequences are serious for the generation of young men and women growing up during this debate. Like everyone else, they form much of their personal identity around their sexuality and gender. One's willingness to listen to and respect the other sex's perspective frames the way a person perceives individual rights and the rights of others. We cannot afford to teach this generation in a way that limits their ability to have compassion for others. If we want this generation and subsequent ones to achieve their best—as individuals and as a group—we need to show them how to respectfully disagree. If we can educate people within this environment of acceptance, I believe it is possible to end the violence that is endemic in our lives.

5

HOW TO MAKE THE SYSTEM
WORK FOR YOU

Unfortunately, no matter how well prepared women are, the risk of assault in their lives is a constant possibility. This chapter will examine the process women go through after an assault. It is a guideline for seeking assistance from the hospital, the police, and the justice system. Because every state, and sometimes every county, has different methods and rules for handling an assault, you need to understand how these institutions function and what options you have within each one. The information presented in this chapter is also a guide for making decisions during this difficult process. There are no right or wrong decisions. Any decision you make is the right one for you because it is yours.

As I have said in previous chapters, I believe it is every woman's obligation to know how to take care of herself. However, there is an important difference between taking responsibility for your actions and blaming yourself after being hurt in a situation that is beyond your control. You can be diligent, use excellent judgment, and still be attacked. You can also live in denial, use horrible judgment, and never be attacked. I hate writing that, but false expectations are very dangerous. No matter how safe you feel, you are at risk of assault. Knowing this, you are responsible for being your own best protector, but you are never to blame for being attacked. Never. No matter what street you walk down, decision you make, alcohol you drink, you are not responsible for being raped or physically assaulted in any way.

If you have been physically or sexually assaulted, you have been through a painful, traumatic experience. While you may feel that you had no control during the attack, you can control the process you go through after the attack. Wishing the emotional pain away will not work; you need help and support. There are people willing and ready to help you, but it is up to you to seek help.

For many women, decision making becomes almost impossible after an assault. But it is right after an assault that your need for good decision making is critical. Naturally, it can be difficult at best to make these decisions, and individual reactions to assault vary. Questions about reporting the crime, getting medical help, counseling, and other issues need to be addressed. As a general rule, if you do nothing else, get medical attention. Overall, never forget that you are entitled to be treated with dignity and respect. If you are not treated in this manner, you have a right to demand it.

IT'S OVER. WHAT DO I DO NOW?

Immediately after an attack, go to a telephone and call a person who can be your "advocate." This person may be a friend, a parent, or a relative. You need someone who is strong-willed, nonjudgmental, and supportive. If you do not have someone like that, call a sexual-assault center (SAC) in your area and ask for an outreach volunteer to come to you. SAC staff people are trained to help people in crisis and answer questions. For example, if you do not know where the best or nearest hospital is located, the crisis center can direct you. You can find a SAC by calling the local operator or police. When your advocate is on the way, call the police. While you are waiting, it is very important that you do not tamper with the crime scene.

The following is a hypothetical situation that illustrates the steps you can take during and after an assault.

> Mary had been reading at 9:00 p.m. in her living room. A man broke into her home and raped her. Although she was terrified and feared for her life during the rape, Mary tried to remember what clothes he was wearing, his height, weight, and other physical characteristics. As soon as he left, Mary went to the window to watch his escape. He jumped into a large gray car and headed north. Although she could not read the license plate, she saw that it was placed inside the car on the left side of the back window. Mary called her sister and then called the police. On the phone she described her attacker's approximate height, weight, and clothes. While she waited for her sister to arrive, she went to the kitchen and wrote down everything she could remember.

During and after an assault like Mary's, it would be very difficult to maintain your calm as she did, but if you can do any one of the things listed above, it will help in catching the attacker. This is especially true if he is a stranger, because establishing his identity is crucial. Try to pay attention to his characteristics. Police Officer Michele Carson of the Cheverly, Maryland, police department offers this advice:

> Look for something that will stand out. Height, race, weight, shoes. Start at the head and go down making mental notes. In a panic it's hard to get a good physical description, but your information is all we have to go on. Don't think that clothes, body odor, or other physical descriptions are not im-

portant. Let's say you tell the police that the assailant was wearing a puffy blue jacket with a tear. Then you say he was a bean pole, and he stank. You also state that you couldn't see what race he was. Then you remembered that when he ran he said, "See ya." This information is given out in roll call. The beat officer is aware of the people in the area and remembers a new face on the block near the pawnshop. When he drives by, there is a short guy and a tall guy dressed in jeans and a T-shirt. The tall man is fair in complexion and looks well groomed. The officer gets out of the car to find out the name of the new face, and the short man walks away. The tall man says, "See ya." As the officer approaches, he notices a bad odor coming from the man. Later the police issue a search warrant for his apartment and find a puffy blue jacket. Case closed. Did the description sound like a lot to go on? No. But does the woman's information get the guy? Yes.

When the attacker leaves, watch to see what direction he takes and his method of transportation. If you decide to call the police, avoid the place where the attack occurred, so that the crime scene remains undisturbed until the police arrive. Officer Carson says:

> When I first get to the place where a woman has been attacked, I see if she's injured and then I check the crime scene. If you need some support until the police arrive, call someone, but don't let them come over and destroy the crime scene. You have saliva, footprints, hairs, fabrics; you may have torn a piece of clothing.

Immediately following an assault, it is natural to want to clean yourself. Unfortunately, you hurt your chances of catching the attacker if you change your physical appearance before receiving medical attention. So even though you really want to bathe, don't. Do not take a shower, brush your hair, brush your teeth, or wash your hands. Do not clean, brush off, or destroy your clothing. If you must change clothes, put the clothes you were wearing in a paper bag and bring them with you to the police station or hospital. (Place your clothes in a paper bag because some substances dissolve in plastic bags.) Avoid drinking any liquid, because it increases your need to urinate. If you do urinate, you are literally washing away the evidence. If you absolutely must, urinate in a jar and bring it with you to the hospital. You need medical attention as soon as possible.

If you are attacked outdoors or in an unfamiliar place, you need to get to a safe place. In chapter 2, I said, "Run to safety, not just away from danger." Think about where you are going before you go. You want to go to a place where you feel comfortable—your home, a family member or friend's home, the hospital, or the local police station. If you are outside and someone passes by, tell the person you have been assaulted. If you can, get the person's name and address, so that if you decide to press charges, s/he can testify about your physical and emotional condition immediately after the assault.

Although I strongly advise calling the police immediately, it is your decision. Many women do not want to call the police, because they assume they have to press charges, they are ashamed, or they blame themselves for the assault. You do not have to press charges if you contact the police after the attack. By reporting, you have informed the police that a crime has occurred. Police officers will briefly question you about the attack and ask if you can describe the attacker. If you want, the police will take you to the hospital.

The Hospital

WHY GO TO THE HOSPITAL?

There are many reasons why you should go to the hospital after an assault. Primarily, you need to be treated for any injuries you may have received. Even if you do not think you have been hurt, you may have suffered internal injuries that are not visible, or you could be in shock and not realize you are physically hurt. Again, if at all possible, wear the clothes you were wearing during the attack, and bring a change of clothes with you. If you cannot wear these clothes to the hospital, place them in a paper bag and bring them with you.

Even if you do not want to press charges initially, the hospital can collect evidence in case you change your mind. Many women do not want to press charges immediately after an assault, because the process seems overwhelming. In some states, medical professionals are required by law to notify the police if they treat a victim of any serious crime, but even if they do, you are not obligated to press charges. You are the only person who can make that decision.

Going to the hospital keeps your legal options open, because you are maintaining your ability to prosecute. It is much easier to go through the medical examination immediately and not press charges than to delay the examination and later decide to press charges. In addition, many states will pay for the exam if you report the attack within thirty-six hours. Hospitals will not give evidential exams more than seventy-two hours after the attack, because most of the evidence will be gone. So if there is even a chance you will want to prosecute, the stronger the medical evidence you have against the attacker, the better your chances for conviction.

After the attack you may be worried about contracting a sexually transmitted disease (STD) or becoming pregnant.

Going to the hospital is the first step in addressing these fears. During the medical examination you can be tested for venereal disease and you can discuss prevention of STDs and pregnancy with your doctor. Follow-up visits will be required to make sure you are healthy, but going to the hospital is your best first step.

WHICH HOSPITAL SHOULD YOU CHOOSE?

It is better to go to a general hospital than to a private physician. Although you may feel more comfortable with your doctor, s/he may be less familiar with the procedures for collecting evidence admissible in court or s/he may not be equipped to perform a gynecological exam to discover internal injuries. Many hospitals have rape-trauma units with a staff trained to deal with the needs of rape survivors. You need to be taken care of by people who can ensure the proper collection of medical evidence and who have experience with sexual assault victims.

WHEN YOU GET TO THE HOSPITAL, WHAT CAN YOU EXPECT?

First of all, you should expect a long wait! Emergency rooms can be very busy, and medical personnel treat people with the most serious injuries first. In order to make the wait more bearable, find a quiet place to sit. If you do not have anyone with you for support, tell the nurses why you are there. In the interviews I have done for this book, I have been told consistently by rape survivors that the nurses were a wonderful support system. I have heard many stories about nurses who continually checked on women to see if they needed a blanket, a private place to rest, or a shoulder to lean on. Most hospitals have a designated room for victims of sexual assault.

If there is none, look for an empty office or a conference room to wait in.

Before the medical examination, you will be asked many questions and you will be required to complete admission and medical history forms. A nurse will need background information (name, birthdate, insurance) and will ask general questions about what happened to you. You do not have to give her details, but you must tell the nurse that you were sexually assaulted. After this information has been obtained, the nurse will give you a consent form so that medical evidence can be collected. You may also be asked for permission to photograph your visible injuries. These photographs can be used as evidence in court.

When you first see the doctor s/he will ask you a series of questions about your current health and medical history. For example, you may be asked if you are allergic to any medications, if you are pregnant, if you have any venereal diseases, what (if any) type of birth control you use, or the date of your last period. Then the doctor will ask personal questions about your sexual behavior and the sexual assault. You may be asked when you last had sexual intercourse prior to the assault, if the attacker ejaculated, if you scratched the attacker, and what sexual acts were performed during the assault (e.g., vaginal, anal, or oral). It is very important that the doctor know exactly what happened to you, so that s/he has a better idea of where and how your injuries occurred and where evidence, like semen, can be found.

WHAT WILL HAPPEN DURING THE MEDICAL EXAM?

You will be taken to a room, given a robe, and asked to undress. If you are wearing the same clothes you had on during the assault, they will be collected, placed in a paper bag, and given to the police as evidence. The fabric of your clothing may contain traces of blood or bodily secretions which could identify the person who attacked you.

The doctor will listen to your heart and lungs, press on your abdomen and back, examine your breasts, and check for general signs of injury. You may be asked to sit on a piece of paper and comb through your pubic hair. The loose hairs that fall onto the paper will be collected, put in an envelope, and kept as evidence. You may also be asked to cut small pieces of your pubic hair and put them in the envelope. The hair will be analyzed for the presence of blood and semen. You may also be asked to pull a few hairs from your head. During an assault, it is common for women to scratch their attacker. For this reason, the doctor may want to scrape under your fingernails for bits of skin, hair, or blood. When all this evidence is collected, it is compared with your blood, hair, and saliva. The foreign substances found on your body will be examined through DNA testing and will help the police identify your attacker in court.

The next step of the medical exam is the pelvic exam. For most women a pelvic exam is uncomfortable even in the best of circumstances. Just remember: it takes only a few minutes, and it has to be done to make sure you are okay. At your request, your advocate or hospital volunteer can stay with you during the examination. But besides the doctor and the nurse, there is no reason for anyone else to be in the room. If there is a police officer in the room and you are not comfortable, ask him/her to leave.

Basically the exam is like a standard gynecological exam that you may have had from your doctor. You will be asked to lie on an examination table with your legs in metal footrests and your knees apart. Almost all women feel somewhat uncomfortable doing this, but it will be easier if you relax by taking deep breaths. Of course, it's almost impossible to relax in that position, but even a slight lessening of tension will help. Just as a side note, the last time I was sitting on a table for my annual pelvic exam, the nurse practitioner assured me she wouldn't say the dreaded "R" word (for relax). When she said that, I laughed and became a little more relaxed. It also helped to close my eyes and talk to her while she examined me, but everyone has her own method for getting through a pelvic exam.

First, the doctor will examine you for any cuts, bruises, and traces of semen outside of the vaginal area. Second, the doctor will insert a metal or plastic speculum into your vagina. If the doctor has not already done so, ask for the speculum to be run under warm water so it won't be so uncomfortable when it is inserted. Once inside, the speculum allows the doctor to open up the internal area of the vagina. The doctor is looking for sperm and other signs of recent intercourse, such as a torn hymen or vaginal or rectal inflammations. If you tell the hospital you wish to report the attack, the doctor will take evidence that will be given to the police. Collecting this evidence is painless and includes wiping cotton swabs over the inside of the vagina. After the doctor has taken this evidence, the speculum will be removed. Evidence may also be taken from your mouth, rectum, or anywhere else dried semen is visible. Third, the doctor will examine you for internal injuries by inserting two fingers into your vagina and placing the other hand on your stomach. The doctor may push gently with her/his hands on your stomach for further examination. The last thing the doctor will do is perform a brief rectal exam by placing one finger in your rectum for a few seconds.

After that, you're done with everything except a few tests. The doctor or nurse will collect urine and blood samples, which will determine whether you are pregnant, carry a sexually transmitted disease (STD), or had any alcohol or drugs in your body at the time of the assault. If you did drink or ingest drugs before you were attacked, you should tell the doctor, because your ability to resist the assault may have been compromised. (This evidence may be helpful if you take your attacker to court. The defense attorney may not be able to argue that you consented to sexual intercourse, because in some states a person whose blood alcohol level is higher than a certain level is considered unable to give consent.) Likewise, if you drank alcohol or took drugs after the attack to calm down, tell the doctor. Not telling the whole truth will only hurt you.

At the end of the examination, you should discuss with the doctor your options for prevention of an unwanted pregnancy and/or sexually transmitted diseases. Although it is unlikely that you would become pregnant from the assault, you have several options. All treatments for the prevention of pregnancy have serious side effects, so it is imperative to understand the known effects of any medication you take. You can also be tested for AIDS. However, an HIV-negative result does not guarantee that you are free from the disease. To be safe, you need to be retested periodically and practice safe sex with your partners.

YOUR MEDICAL RIGHTS

One of the most common reactions to an assault is the feeling of total helplessness: you were not in control. Frequently a woman's feelings of helplessness are compounded when she goes to the police and/or hospital, because she must again relinquish control to the hospital staff or police officers. Therefore, it is very important that you know your rights. Overall, you have the right to walk out of the hospital at any time. These people are supposed to be there to help you; you are under no obligation to anyone but yourself.

Remember, during the examination you have the right to have a friend, social worker, or relative with you. You also have the right to total privacy while you are being treated in the emergency room. You can ask anyone, including police officers, to leave, except the medical personnel necessary for the examination. If a police officer is required to be present for legal reasons, you can request a female officer.

When you receive the medical evidence, it is up to you what to do with it. You can also decide not to have the evidence collected, even if you requested venereal and pregnancy tests. And you can choose whether or not to give the results of the exam to the police. You can receive copies of the report and demand that they remain confidential. You can also refuse to have photographs taken of your injuries. But remember, photographs may help catch your attacker. If you are uncomfortable about having this done but want the pictures, ask a female officer to take them. After your hospital exam is completed and you have filled out a report with the police, the police can drive you home or anywhere you would like to go.

PAYING YOUR MEDICAL BILLS

Your first source of reimbursement is any medical insurance you may have. If you do not have insurance or are unable to pay your share of the expenses, you have some options. Many states have victim-assistance programs that will reimburse you for the medical, emotional, or financial losses you have suffered as a result of the assault. But in order to be eligible for this compensation, most states require that you report the crime to law enforcement officials. Keep all records of your bills, receipts, and canceled checks in order to document your claim. To find out if your state has a victim-assistance program, call your district attorney's office, or local rape-crisis center.

The Police

As soon as you are raped and seek help, you are involved in a long process. But it is worth it. The attack was not your fault, and your attacker needs to be held accountable.
Cheryl Banks, Director,
Prince Georges County Sexual Assault Trauma Center

I have seen many types of sexual assault, including ones against prostitutes. I don't care if a person sells her body for a living. I base my opinion on the fact that the person said no. Then I work hard to prove force, threat, fear, and other elements needed to convict . . . I pray that all police officers realize that they have a serious responsibility to the citizen, because the success of the case depends on the professionalism of the officer assigned.
Police Officer Michele Carlson, Cheverly Police Department,
Prince Georges County

Every woman handles the decision to report her assault to the police differently. Some women immediately decide that they will press charges and do everything in their power to put their attacker in jail. Others decide that they will not press charges. And some women decide one course of action and later change their mind. In Cheryl Banks's opinion,

Calling the police should be left up to the woman, but at least she needs to know her options. Gather the evidence for yourself, and figure out where you are in your life . . . Is this something you can do? Maybe at that moment, reporting is something you just can't do. Personally, I would like everyone to report a rape to the police because men tend to rape again, and for a woman it can be very empowering to stand up and say, "You can't do this to me."

Any decision you make during this process is a valid one. It is completely understandable for a woman not to press charges immediately following an assault but to decide to press charges later, when she feels less traumatized.

If at all possible, I think you should report the rape. According to the Justice Department's 1992 report on violence against women, perpetrators of rape and sexual assault have the highest repeat-offense rate of any criminals in our country. Rapists are not people who rape once—i.e., because they lose control if a woman is dressed provocatively. If you do not report the rape, there is no way the attacker will be caught or held accountable for his crime, and it is very likely that he will rape again. If you do report it, you will be fighting back against the injustice you suffered, and there is a chance that you will have saved another woman from this brutal experience. Your report could also substantiate the claim of other women who have been assaulted. With each reported crime, the police have a better chance of catching the rapist. Also, when you report the crime, you inform the police that there is a rapist in your community. Your report may lead to an increased number of patrol cars in your area and enable the police to provide better protection for your community.

Some women feel that reporting the crime is the first step in taking back control of their lives. It can be an empowering experience. Making the report and going through the judicial process can be frightening, but facing that fear and persevering is a reward all its own. Rapists need to be held accountable for their actions, and you can be instrumental in bringing this about. However, the reality is that most women do not report the crime, because they believe nothing will be done about it. Many women do not trust the police and are afraid of being judged or treated badly, or of not being believed. Christina's comment reflects what many women feel when they go through the reporting process:

> The police asked me to take a lie-detector test. Two weeks after I was raped I got pneumonia; I was in no condition to take the test, so I put it off. In August the detective called me and said, "Christina, if you don't take the lie-detector test, we are going to have to close the case." I didn't take it. I was really frightened. I thought they would ask me questions that had nothing to do with the rape and that would brand me a liar. I was really scared that I was being put on trial and wouldn't be believed.

Christina's feelings explain why so many women do not report a sexual assault. In addition to dealing with your emotional state, you have to tell your story repeatedly to police officers and in court. This is not easy to do once, let alone many times.

However, I think the worst fear women have in reporting a sexual assault is that the attacker will retaliate. This fear is natural in light of the fact that an estimated 75 percent of attackers warn their victims not to tell the police. If you are faced with this situation, you must make a choice: either remain silent and let your life continue to be dominated by fear, or fight back by learning to defend yourself and using the justice system to your advantage.

If you initially decide not to report, you can still change your mind. Many women think that there is no way to successfully press charges if you wait. That is not true, but there are some additional problems. The police will have a harder time trusting you if you do not report the crime immediately. Your evidence loses strength in court, and the attorney for the accused rapist may use your delay against you. But reporting late is better than not reporting at all, and the assailant can still be convicted. Even if you think your case is really weak in the eyes of the law, it can still be prosecuted and won. As Police Officer Michele Carlson said:

> Sometimes I am surprised by the cases I win. I had a case where an unemployed woman, who was on welfare, had three illegitimate children, and was about to be evicted from her apartment, went downstairs to get her mail. A man with a knife forced her back upstairs. He was in her apartment for two and a half hours. He played with her children, made long-distance telephone calls, and raped her. The knife was the only evidence, because her neighbor had come over after the rape and by the time the police arrived the crime scene was destroyed. The rapist had called a taxi from her apartment, and we were able to trace it. We won that case.

REPORTING PROCEDURES

If you decide to report the attack to the police, it will be easier if you know what to expect. Reporting an assault involves calling the police or going to the police station, describing the incident by giving a statement, and working to identify your attacker (sometimes by helping a police artist compose a sketch of him). If the first police officers you talk to are patrol officers, keep in mind that some do not come into contact with rape victims often. As a result, they tend to be less sensitive than police officers who work with sexual-assault victims. If they are not sensitive, keep in mind that you have done nothing wrong. You have the right to demand better treatment, but give them the chance to help. Just remember, they are people too. Cheryl Banks gives this advice:

> Go with the police officer you have until (s)he proves you wrong. When I train police officers, one of the things that strikes me is that many of them have already had personal

experiences with rape. One trainee told me that his wife was a rape survivor. So just because an officer is male does not mean that he is going to be insensitive. Many times they are scared, too.

On the flip side, sometimes women are so angry with their attacker that they vent their rage on the police officers. The police are there to help you; they are not the enemy. Police Officer Michele Carlson says, "Try not to be frustrated with the police officer. Many women are angry because we were not there to stop the assault. We walk in with our gun, badge, and uniform, taking charge after the assault has happened and the bad guy is gone." Sensitive, educated officers understand this and take these feelings into account during the interview.

Police officers will meet a rape victim at the scene of the crime, at the police station, or at the hospital. If you contact the police right after the attack, they are responsible for taking you to the hospital for a medical examination. Initially you will be asked general questions about the assault—your name, address, age, what happened, and a description of the attacker. Before an investigation proceeds, the police are required to determine if there is reasonable cause to believe that a rape occurred. I know I have said this before, but it is worth saying again: The more forthright you are about the assault, the more credible you will be to the police. Inaccurate or incorrect information may cause the police to follow false leads. If your story is inconsistent, the police may doubt you are telling the truth. If you do not remember something or are unsure, say so directly.

After the medical examination the police will ask you to give a more detailed report. This report can be given at either the hospital or the police station. Most of the rape survivors I have spoken with were taken to the police station for further questioning. Giving this detailed report can be very difficult.

Again, the police officer may prefer to interview you alone, but you can have your advocate with you. You have the right to request a female officer, but your request may result in a delay in the reporting procedure, because some police agencies may not have female officers readily available. Whoever interviews you could ask hundreds of questions and ask you to repeat your story many times. It is easy to perceive this line of questioning as insensitive and distrustful, but the police are trying to ascertain all the facts. They ask you to repeat things so that you can remember everything that happened to you. Some of the questions may be highly embarrassing; but remember, the person who attacked you did these things, not you. The police will want to know if penetration occurred and what sexual acts were forced upon you. No matter how embarrassing it may be, tell the police everything that happened, because only in this way can they determine what crimes have been committed. Some of the questions will seem irrelevant. For example, they may ask if the assailant was left- or right-handed. Did he apologize? Did he use a lubricant? As most rapists are repeat offenders, the police are asking specific questions that tie your attacker to other crimes. All these questions are asked so that the investigating officer can write his/her report, which is crucial to the outcome of your case. If the report is thorough and complete, your chance to successfully prosecute your attacker substantially increases. Police officers know this and usually spend considerable time on each report.

In some states, where the victim's sexual history can be taken into account in court, the police investigator may ask questions pertaining to your character. This will happen in states that do not have rape shield laws, which limit or restrict the kind of information the defense can use about the victim. Federal rape shield law 412 states that the accused cannot get on the stand or put anyone else on the stand to give evidence about the alleged victim's past sexual history. In states that do have rape shield laws, personal questions may still be asked in cases involving marital or date rape. It is understandably upsetting to answer questions like that—especially in the circumstances where they are being presented. You could be asked: How many men have you slept with? Do you go to singles' bars often? Do you frequently get picked up? Unfortunately, if you refuse to answer these questions, you jeopardize your case by becoming less believable in the eyes of the police.

If you know your attacker, the police may pick him up for

RAPE SHIELD LAWS

In some states the defense can ask you questions about your sexual history and/or character. However, many states have recently enacted rape shield laws that limit or restrict the kind of information the defense can seek about the complaining witness (the victim). These laws attempt to strike a responsible balance between the victim's right to her privacy and the defendant's right to information that could be relevant to his case. The best description I have seen of rape shield laws and their guidelines is in Linda Fairstein's book, *Sexual Violence: Our War Against Rape*. She describes five situations in which the defense may use the victim's personal history:

1. The victim and the accuser have had prior sexual relations. This takes into consideration the context of the relationship and the events that brought them together when the supposed attack took place.
2. The victim has been convicted of prostitution within the past three years. Ironically, this rule actually helps the prosecutor because it limits the questions the defense can ask. Before this rule was in effect, the defense was allowed to ask witnesses if they had ever worked as prostitutes. Without any evidence to support the question, the defense would try to plant doubt in the jury about the victim's reputation and credibility. This is not to say that prostitutes cannot be raped. In fact, prostitutes are frequently victims of rape, they do have the right to press charges against someone, and their cases can be successfully prosecuted.

RAPE SHIELD LAWS (*cont.*)

3. The prosecutor claims the victim was "chaste" (had never had sexual intercourse), and the defense has evidence to the contrary.

4. The prosecutor attempts to prove that the victim contracted a venereal disease or became pregnant as a result of the attack. The defense is then allowed to bring in specific evidence to rebut the prosecutor's claim.

5. The court determines that the victim's personal history is "relevant and admissible in the interest of justice." While this general exception could be used to render rape shield laws completely ineffective, Ms. Fairstein reports that this exception has never been used in New York and is used infrequently in other courts around the country.

In your state, rape shield laws may be applied differently or may not be used at all. If you are in a situation where your personal and/or sexual history will be brought up at trial, it is absolutely understandable to be upset and angry. Unfortunately, if you refuse to answer these questions, you jeopardize your case by appearing less believable.

questioning. If the attacker is a stranger, the police will investigate other cases and follow up on clues left by him. Most police stations have files of photographs or mug shots that you can look through to identify the attacker. If the police apprehend him, you may be asked to attend a lineup. The participants in a lineup are allowed to alter their appearance—they can shave, change their hairstyle, or wear different clothes, but they can't see you. If the attacker is caught and identified, then the case is turned over to the prosecutor.

I know that in the short term, reporting the crime to the police can seem frightening, and, no matter what, there is no guarantee that it will be a positive experience. But you have to give yourself and the system a chance to work. If you don't report, there is no chance of your attacker being brought to justice. You are not the first woman to be physically or sexually assaulted, and you will not be the last. Make your attacker responsible for his actions. Do not let him think he can continue without consequences.

YOUR RIGHTS

Just as you have rights at the hospital, you have rights when dealing with the police. You have the right to read over everything the officers write on forms or in your report, and you can ask them to correct any misinformation. As an overall rule, it's best to get the names, badge numbers, serial numbers, and business telephone numbers of any officers involved in your case. You have the right to request a copy of your police report, and you have the right to make a report and not proceed with prosecution.

If you are interviewed by a police officer who behaves in a hostile, inappropriate, or patronizing manner, do not continue the interview. His/her behavior has nothing to do with you. Unfortunately, some police officers may doubt women who report a rape because they have filed reports from other women who subsequently dropped the charges or made false claims. Police Officer Michele Carlson says:

> There are different kinds of police officers. There are those who bring their home problems to work with them. Then there are those who are very compassionate and really care about solving the victim's problems. I have seen police officers who are impatient and bully the victims. From talking with male officers, I have found that some of them take offense when the victim does not cooperate, because they want to come to her rescue and help so badly. Others just don't understand; they believe that the victim is wasting their time.

When you are up against this type of officer, ask to speak to the supervisor or the sergeant. Do not get into an argument with him or her. Just sit down, compose yourself, and wait. It is really important to have a good investigating officer, because if you don't and you get angry, there is a chance you will get flustered and won't clearly remember the crime.

If you do have a hostile officer, your advocate can really help. Especially if your advocate is from the local SAC, she can make sure that the officer is reported to the proper personnel at the local police station. Or, if you are ever asked to be an advocate for someone and you have a problem, ask to speak to the police officer alone and tell him/her that the best way to get the statement s/he needs is to exercise more patience and sensitivity.

The Court

Historically rape has often been difficult to prove in the American legal system for a number of reasons. First, until very recently, the law has been written and interpreted by men. Thus, it has been difficult for women to access and successfully use the legal system. Second, conviction depends on finding guilt "beyond a reasonable doubt." Since conviction is frequently dependent on an alleged rapist's word against his victim's, it is often difficult to convince the judge or jury that rape occurred—it could merely be a difference of perceptions. So what do you need to know if you want to use the legal system to prosecute a sexual assault? The following section will provide some of this information.

Although the prosecuting process can differ by state, there are some basic laws you can expect. Once you report and press charges, you become a witness for the state. Rape is viewed as a crime against the state. You are not the plaintiff;

you are the state's witness. This is not unique to rape and/or assault cases; all crimes are handled this way. Consequently, neither the district attorney (DA) nor the police have the responsibility of informing you about the progress of your case. You can request information, but they are not obligated to provide it. However, the prosecuting attorneys I have spoken with say that they do inform the victim of changes in the case. Many district attorneys believe that they have a moral obligation to provide information to the victim as it becomes available.

Prosecuting your case is the responsibility of the prosecutor's office. At all times you have the right to have your own attorney present. Your case will be handled according to the prosecutor's jurisdiction (laws vary by state). You could have the same prosecutor throughout the case, or it could be handled by different prosecutors as it proceeds.

Typically, if the suspect is arrested, the police present the case to the district attorney, or prosecutor, who then decides whether there is sufficient evidence to issue a formal complaint. If the district attorney believes there is insufficient evidence, your case will be rejected. Rejection does not always mean that the district attorney doesn't believe a rape occurred. Knowing how difficult the court system can be, a district attorney may not want to put a woman through the trouble if she is going to lose. In the words of Los Angeles Deputy District Attorney Mary Hanlon, "I'm not going to put a victim on trial just to be eaten alive." It is common for women whose cases are rejected to be angry with the district attorney. If you have this experience and you really believe that your case is strong enough to proceed, ask the district attorney to clearly explain why s/he rejected the case. If you still believe the case is strong, you can ask his or her supervisor to review the case.

One of the most critical elements in the successful outcome of your case is your honesty with the district attorney. Even if there is something you are embarrassed about or feel would damage your credibility, tell the truth. If you don't, there is a good chance the defense attorney will find out about it and use it against you, and the district attorney could easily lose your case. If the district attorney is prepared, s/he can minimize its ability to hurt the case. In addition, things you may be embarrassed about may not be so bad. Another Los Angeles district attorney, Phil Stirling, says, "Juries want to hear that you are human. And if a woman is not honest, it will come back to haunt her." For District Attorney Mary Hanlon the most frustrating aspect of her job is when witnesses don't tell her the truth. "I try to do everything for a woman, and then sometimes she doesn't tell the truth. The verdict does not hinge on your being the perfect person . . . We won't reject the case if you didn't fight to the death or have something in your past you are ashamed of."

The district attorney also decides what charges will be brought against the suspect. These can include rape, forced oral copulation, sexual assault, robbery, or kidnapping, to name a few. If formal charges are made, the suspect is held until the preliminary examination, which should not exceed a "reasonable time" after the arrest. The time limit depends on the state in which the case is being heard.

The preliminary hearing is usually short—only the basic details of the case are disclosed. The district attorney's goal in the preliminary hearing is to establish probable cause that the assault occurred and that the suspect committed the crime without your consent. S/he does this by presenting evidence and giving your testimony to a judge or jury. Again, depending on the state, you may be required to attend this hearing.

If the judge or jury finds that there is insufficient evidence to establish cause or that the accused person's rights were violated, the suspect is released. Your only recourse is to file a civil suit against your attacker. If probable cause is established, the accused is held and arraigned on the indictment before a judge. At arraignment, the accused is notified of the charges against him, read his rights, and allowed to enter a plea. If he cannot afford his own attorney, the court appoints an attorney to defend him.

If the accused pleads not guilty, a date is set for pretrial motions and the judge will consider releasing the accused on bail until the trial. You have no say in the amount of bail that is set. Depending on the state, bail will be set proportional to the judge's determination of the defendant's danger to you and/or the community and/or the accused's ties to the community. For example, if the accused has a full-time job and family, a low bail may be set because he is not likely to run away. If you have any concerns about your safety until the trial, discuss them with the district attorney and s/he will present your concerns to the judge.

If the accused pleads guilty, a date is set for sentencing. If you like, you can issue a victim-impact statement to the judge, which describes how the assault has affected you. This can influence the sentencing decision.

The pretrial period can be long. It is not uncommon for numerous delays to come up before the trial actually begins. Defense attorneys use these delays in the hope that the state will drop the charges if witnesses move, die, or are unable to testify, or if memories fade. Don't let this discourage you. During the waiting period, keep up with the status of your case, but don't put your life on hold. Before the trial, you will meet with the district attorney to review your testimony and be advised of courtroom procedures. If you have any questions about your case or anything in general, this is a good time to ask.

When the trial finally begins, you will probably be nervous. Just remember, you are not the person who did anything wrong. By taking the accused to trial, you are doing something right for yourself and for all women. The attacker was the one who did something wrong. Many people feel intimidated in court, so just relax and do the best you can. Many prosecutors prepare witnesses by having them practice their testimony, review defense strategies, and visit the courtroom to familiarize themselves with the court environment.

The accused has the right to choose a trial by jury or a trial by judge. Most likely the defendant will choose a jury trial, because juries often carry biases and believe the traditional myths about rape—that is, the woman was asking for it or teased him. With a judge, one person decides. With a jury, if only one person votes not guilty, the result is a hung jury and the defendant is not convicted. The defense hopes to use the jury's biases to the defendant's advantage during the trial. In order for the jury to convict the accused, they must believe he is guilty "beyond a reasonable doubt." The accused also has the option of testifying on his own behalf. If he has a record of past offenses, he will probably not testify, because if the accused chooses not to testify, his record of past offenses is inadmissible. The accused may testify if his defense is that you falsely identified him, if he has an alibi, or if he claims you consented to having sex.

Until it is your time to testify, you will not be allowed in the courtroom, because you are considered a witness and could thus be influenced by other evidence or testimony. Your testimony will begin when you are asked to give your oath to tell the truth. After giving your oath, you will be asked by the district attorney to tell your story. The district attorney will ask you questions during your testimony to clarify your statements and/or add details.

After the district attorney has completed your direct testimony, you will be cross-examined by the defense attorney. The cross-examination is used to try to discredit your testimony and to create a reasonable doubt in the jury's mind. There are some basic strategies defense attorneys use in their attempts to do this:

1. *False identification.* The defense attorney charges that you or the police have accused the wrong person of the crime. This strategy is used most often when the attacker is a stranger.

2. *Consent.* The defense attorney admits sexual contact occurred but argues that you consented to the act. This strategy is often used in date/acquaintance-rape situations, where there is a prior relationship between the people involved. This information will most likely be used to establish a pattern of consent. These are also the cases where your sexual history is brought up by the defense. In most states there are restrictions on the kinds of questions that can be asked about past sexual history (see page 140). For example, in California a witness's prior history can be used only if there is a history of sexual conduct with the defendant or if the witness has previously been found to have accused someone falsely of rape.

3. *Your behavior.* The defense may question your behavior before the assault and argue that your behavior indicated consent. This relates directly to the myth that men can't control themselves and are therefore not responsible for their actions when faced with an "alluring" woman.

4. *Jealousy.* The defense may also try to make the accused look like the victim of a vindictive, obsessed, or jealous woman.

After you testify, you are allowed to stay in the courtroom for the remainder of the trial. After all the evidence and testimony have been presented, the district attorney and the defense attorney will summarize their arguments. After the summaries comes the verdict.

THE VERDICT AND SENTENCING

In order for the accused to be found guilty in a jury trial, the verdict must be unanimous. Even if the judge or jury believe the accused is probably guilty, they cannot find him guilty if they have a reasonable doubt. A not-guilty verdict does not mean that the judge or jury did not believe a rape occurred. A not-guilty verdict means that the district attorney failed to conclusively make the case, and the defense attorney was successful in establishing reasonable doubt. If the verdict is not-guilty, then the accused is set free and cannot be tried again for the same crime. If the accused is found guilty, he will be held, and a date for sentencing will be set. In spite of all the frustrations and difficulties in trying a case, a woman can win, and the experience can be very rewarding. "The joy of being a DA is when we get a conviction," says District Attorney Hanlon. "It makes me feel good to see the relief the victim feels when the defendant is sent away. She feels validated, and there is a sense of justice."

The judge decides what sentence the accused will be given, and it is up to you to be there for sentencing. The sentence can vary according to state law, sentencing requirements, specifics of the case, and the charge. As in the preliminary hearing, you can read aloud or submit a victim-impact statement to the judge in order to influence his/her decision.

Your case could end at any time during this process for one of two reasons: it is labeled unfounded, or the accused enters into a plea bargain. If your case is termed unfounded, it does not mean that rape did not occur or that you were not believed. An unfounded case is one that the police believe is not strong enough or that the district attorney believes could not be won in court. Some reasons for weak cases include: a delay in reporting; a prior relationship between you and the accused; and the absence of a weapon during the rape. As you can see, this describes the majority of acquaintance/date-rape attacks. If your case is deemed unfounded and you want to complain, you can write to the police or the district attorney's supervisor, who can override the decision. Another option is to hire your own lawyer and pursue a civil case against the accused, but for many women this is prohibitively expensive. The case may also be dropped if the suspect cannot be found or the victim is unwilling to cooperate with the prosecuting attorneys.

The other possible end of your case is a plea bargain. A plea agreement can be made between the district attorney and the defense lawyer anytime before a verdict is handed down. They are not required to inform you of their plea decisions, but many do. If the case is not strong, the district attorney may accept a plea on the condition that the defendant spend a reasonable time incarcerated. Usually in a plea agreement, the accused is required to plead guilty to some or all of the charges in exchange for a predetermined, usually reduced sentence. He can agree to plead guilty to certain charges if other charges are dropped, or he can plead guilty to a less serious offense than the one he is being charged with.

CIVIL SUITS

You can file a civil suit anytime during the criminal proceedings. It can be initiated before you know the outcome of the criminal proceedings. However, be aware that the statute of limitations (the amount of time you have to file the case) and the requirements vary from state to state. Civil suits differ from criminal suits in many important ways. The burden of proof is less stringent. The jury's decision does not have to be unanimous, and the defendant's guilt is determined by a "preponderance of evidence" rather than "beyond a reasonable doubt." Your testimony is sufficient evidence to win the case, so proof of injuries you suffered or medical reports are not mandatory. In addition, any perceived "victim misconduct" (i.e., you "teased" him by your dress and/or behavior) is not relevant.

You can also file a third-party civil suit. This is the same as a civil suit except that you are suing a third party for allowing the assault to occur. For example, if you were attacked in a garage, you may be able to sue the owner if the garage was unsafe (no clear exit signs, improper lighting, etc.). In order to successfully win a third-party lawsuit, you must show that the third party was negligent and failed in their duty and responsibility to protect from unreasonable risk a person for whom they were in some way responsible.

Remember, this chapter should be used only as a guideline, because rules vary according to the jurisdiction in which the assault took place. But in spite of these differences, there are some constants: decisions and responses to an assault are up to the survivor. If she wants to seek medical assistance, report the crime, or prosecute, she is entitled to be treated with dignity and respect. It is my intention that the information in this chapter make the reporting process a little easier to understand and therefore more likely to be used. I truly hope that if you are ever faced with the decision to report an assault, you will do so, because there is a chance justice will be served.

6

THE LONG JOURNEY:
THE RECOVERY PROCESS AFTER
A RAPE

Self-respect, confidence, respect for others, taking care of oneself, boundaries, self-love, appreciation. After the rape, these concepts were not handed to me—I struggled to find them, and when I finally got them, it didn't mean I would know how to put them into practice.

Catie, a sixteen-year-old rape survivor

Recovering from the rape means listening to my instincts, protecting myself, being aware of my role in relationships, taking responsibility for my mistakes, respecting other people's boundaries, respecting my personal boundaries, and being able to risk rejection for healthy, loving relationships with men and women.

Catie, two years later

Picking up the pieces of your life after an assault can be the most difficult challenge you ever face. In a relatively short period of time your most fundamental beliefs can be shattered, your sense of bodily integrity, security, and basic justice can be destroyed, and you may question your most important, intimate relationships. But in spite of all this, your life will continue, and it is up to you to put the pieces back together. As much as you might like to forget the whole thing, it has become part of you. Therefore, the way you respond and take care of yourself after the attack can have a significant impact on the quality of your future life. So how do you get through this process? This chapter is intended to help, but healing is a continuous journey. No matter which path you choose, the guiding principle should be to attempt to reach a point where you can express your feelings, live with the memories of your experience, and integrate them into your identity in a way that you acknowledge and accept.

I don't think it's possible to "heal" from a rape in the traditional sense of healing. It is not like breaking an arm: once you set the arm in a cast, the bone heals, and soon you are as good as new. Recovery from rape is more like being cut. As you heal and time passes, the cut becomes less visible under the layers of skin that grow over it, but you can always see it. I think the connotation of "healing" is inadequate when dealing with sexual assault. It can easily set up false assumptions and expectations that survivors will someday be able to put the ordeal completely behind them. In my own experience, I felt bad for years because I couldn't understand why I continued to think about my relationship long after it ended. I was ashamed that I couldn't simply get over it and leave it behind me. I thought I had a personal weakness that prohibited me from ever "healing." I have finally learned that the recovery process after any kind of traumatic abuse and/ or assault means accepting that you have had an experience you will carry with you. The pain forces you to face yourself more honestly than you thought possible or necessary. And through that pain you can learn a great deal about yourself. It can be a touchstone for you as you face future challenges.

This chapter will provide information on common emotional and mental responses after an assault, the way a survivor's relationships with friends, lovers, and family are affected, and some coping skills to begin the recovery process. All the ideas about the healing process should not be taken as definitive. Rather, "they are an attempt to impose simplicity and order on a process that is inherently turbulent and complex."* More than anything else presented in this book, this information should be used as a guide. If your reaction to a sexual assault is different from the ones I discuss, there is nothing wrong with you. The following outline is based on general assumptions about reactions to traumatic experiences, but we each have individual reactions when we experience terror and powerlessness.

RAPE-TRAUMA SYNDROME

Rape-Trauma Syndrome is an acute stress reaction to a completed or attempted sexual assault. It describes possible responses to an assault, which vary with each individual. There are two major phases: the immediate phase, when the survivor's daily routine is completely disrupted, and the long-term phase, when the survivor strives to reorganize her life.

First Phase: Confusion
1. Shock and/or disbelief; why did it happen to me?
2. Denial. This can manifest itself in a number of ways. The survivor may focus on the emotions of her loved ones instead of her own and/or explain the attack in a flat nonemotional tone of voice
3. Control. In an attempt to reassert control after the attack, the survivor may try to restrain her emotions by denying her pain or by minimizing the effect of the attack
4. Intense mood swings
5. Fear that others will think differently of her if they know she has been attacked
6. Fear of retaliation by her attacker

---

* Judith Lewis Herman, *Trauma and Recovery: The Aftermath of Violence—From Domestic Abuse to Political Terror* (New York: HarperCollins, 1992), p. 133.

RAPE-TRAUMA SYNDROME (*cont.*)

7. Difficulty maintaining concentration or confusion about making any kind of decisions. It is common for a survivor to pick through her memories of the attack, looking for behavior that placed her at risk. If poor judgment is found, it's not a large leap for the rape survivor to believe that any decision she makes in the future will be bad or will place her at greater risk

8. Fear and apprehension concerning any sexual interaction

9. Concern about sexually transmitted diseases, pregnancy, or injury

10. Fear that no one will believe her

11. Self-blame. There are a number of reasons why a survivor chooses to blame herself for an assault: if she can identify what she did to bring on the attack, then she knows she can change her behavior and reduce her risk of being raped again

12. Difficulty being alone and sleeping; nightmares

Second Phase: Trying to Reorganize

After the immediate reaction to the attack wanes, many women try to reorganize their daily routine. It is a way of reasserting control and taking the first steps away from the immediate pain of the assault. Possible reactions may be:

1. Fear of any environment or of people that somehow remind her of the assault

2. Changing her daily routine or residence

3. Ending relationships with friends, lovers, or family members and/or beginning new relationships

4. Distrust of others

Third Phase: Integration

During this phase the rape survivor attempts to integrate her feelings and reactions to the attack while resuming her daily life. When this is achieved, she has reached the final phase of her recovery process and

RAPE-TRAUMA SYNDROME (*cont.*)

1. Feels safe and in control
2. Places the blame on the assailant, not on herself
3. Regains a sense of normalcy
4. Expresses and resolves feelings of fear and rage

POST-TRAUMATIC STRESS DISORDER

Post-traumatic Stress Disorder is a multifaceted, complex re-action to psychological trauma. For our purposes, we will keep it relatively simple. The concept of Post-traumatic Stress Disorder is helpful because it describes how human beings, not just women, generally respond when they witness or experience extreme violence, terror, and powerlessness. It takes into account the belief that people develop in ways which make them rely on a few certainties—that there is a particular order and character to human relationships (at the very least, you expect others to recognize that you are a human being); that one has control over one's body; and that there is a sense of basic justice in the world. When these certainties are chal-lenged or destroyed, any individual will respond in a com-plicated and painful way.

Most women who have been raped report that they believed their lives were in danger during the assault. As we have discussed earlier, the act of rape often confirms a woman's worst fear: that when her life is in danger, it is possible to be totally powerless to alter the course of events. Faced with this situation, the body and mind respond in a series of com-plicated ways based on the person's feeling of "intense fear, helplessness, loss of control, and threat of annihilation."* In

* Herman, *Trauma and Recovery*, p. 155.

general, responses to a rape fall into three categories: (1) *hyperarousal*, where the person anticipates danger at all times, regardless of the environment; (2) *intrusion*, where the person has an indelible image of the trauma in her mind and repeats this image over and over again; and (3) *constriction*, where the person numbs all feeling in response to the sense of total surrender she experienced during the assault.

Hyperarousal means that after a woman has experienced an assault, she is constantly on the lookout for danger, whether she is asleep or awake. Not surprisingly, it can also be very difficult for her to get any kind of rest. She will have extreme responses to unexpected noises, sights, or sensations as well as an intense reaction to anything that reminds her of the trauma. Basically, think of a person who is constantly on the alert. Catie, a woman who survived a brutal rape by a skinhead, describes her experience immediately after the attack:

> Almost overnight, I went from being very social to being very introverted. If anyone touched me, I felt as if I were receiving an electric shock. Everyone seemed like an intruder, and if anyone came too close, I would jump. I felt that any boundaries I had before the rape were destroyed.

In *intrusion*, a traumatized person relives the event as though it were continually recurring in the present. She cannot resume the normal course of her life, because the trauma repeatedly interrupts it. It is as if time stopped at the moment of the trauma, and the images can't be shaken. During the intrusion phase, it is common to have terrifying and repetitive nightmares and flashbacks. (Later in this chapter, both are more fully explained.)

During *constriction*, the person shuts down, freezes, or goes into a different level of consciousness. In some ways, this coping mechanism may be an attempt to slowly deal with the overwhelming emotional pain the rape has caused. In Catie's words,

> When I was raped, I was alone. I was numb and would have been had everyone hugged me, told me that the rape wasn't my fault, listened to me, or sat with me. I like to think I would have cried—but I couldn't. I even felt guilty because I didn't feel anything.

Coping with these reactions can be made more difficult because they often occur simultaneously, and you may feel pulled apart as a result. "[The survivor] finds herself caught between floods of intense, overwhelming feeling and arid states of no feeling at all, between irritable, impulsive action and complete inhibition of action. The instability produced by these periodic alterations further exacerbates the traumatized person's sense of unpredictability and helplessness."* Or, in a rape survivor's words, "It's not really a series of stages. You feel as though you are constantly going back and forth between them."

COPING/SURVIVAL STRATEGIES

We have discussed some ways in which people respond to an assault. There are also steps they can take to begin the road to recovery. The immediate need is to feel safe. After your physical security is ensured, you can begin the process of acknowledging pain and anger, and then fit this experience and the feelings it has caused into your life story.

The recovery process is generally divided into three stages, which can exist separately or in conjunction with one another. The first phase is establishing physical safety. The second phase is recognizing and acknowledging your feelings. And

---

* Herman, *Trauma and Recovery*, p. 175.

the third phase is reconnecting with "normal" life. Although these are distinctive stages, they do not have to take place sequentially. You may be working out your feelings in the second phase and, at the same time, going through a period when you feel unsafe and need to take steps to better protect yourself. Or, while you are attempting to reconnect, feelings that need attention may be brought to the surface. Christina comments:

> I think that the three stages of recovery are constantly at work. It is unfair to say that you go through a set series of stages. I am constantly trying to make my life safer and to feel more in control . . . You can't predict how a rape survivor will feel. It is up to the individual and how much she is able to handle at any given time. I think the only thing that I can say about healing and recovery is that it takes time, perseverance, and patience.

Overall, it's most important to allow yourself to go through all these elements of recovery as they occur. You will probably not experience each phase distinctly, so don't get frustrated if you feel as if you are going backwards in the recovery process or you are "revisiting" a phase.

ESTABLISHING SAFETY

In the immediate aftermath of an attack, you need to take steps to increase your sense of physical safety. First, you must reestablish control over your own body. Whether or not you wish to report the crime to the police, it is very important that you seek immediate medical attention. This means being examined after the rape for possible sexually transmitted diseases (STDs) or injuries. As much as you are able, try to sleep, eat, and do basic physical exercise. Second, set up a safe living situation, financial security, mobility, and a plan for self-protection within your daily routine. A good example of establishing a safer living environment is Anne's move to a new apartment and her insistence on increased security measures.

> The apartment I moved into following my rape was the second floor of a group house. At the time I moved in, there were no outside lights on the house, no dead bolts on the doors, no locks on the bedroom doors, and no screens on the windows ... I went on a crusade with my landlady to address my safety concerns. Lights, dead bolts, locks, and screens were added, and I felt comfortable because I felt safer.

Another rape survivor I interviewed was attacked in her car, so naturally she was afraid to get into any car. To overcome her fear, she visualized being in a car in a safe environment. When she was comfortable with that, she had a friend help her into the car and then they drove around. A few days later she went back to the car with her friend, but this time she drove. She overcame her fear because she identified it and then took steps to regain the feeling of being in control of her own movements.

Most of all, be kind to yourself. Experiencing a sexual assault can call into question your independence and your belief in your body's integrity. Think about your unique personal strengths, and list them on a piece of paper for easy reference. Were there times before the attack when you faced a stressful situation? If so, how did you handle it? Think about your strengths, and have the confidence that those strengths will assist you again. Even symptoms or behavior that may appear strange can be effective coping mechanisms. And don't be embarrassed about sharing your fears with others. If you need to check the closets ten times before going to bed and leave all the lights on, that's fine. Don't ignore or dismiss your feelings. Examine, acknowledge, and address them. Otherwise, when feelings are repressed, they can continue to haunt you for years. A rape survivor relates her struggle:

> I was determined that I wasn't going to let the rape affect my feelings about sexual intercourse. But that didn't happen. Three years later I'm still dealing with these issues. Right after the rape I had sex to prove to myself that the rape wasn't bothering me. I also put myself in dangerous situations to prove to myself that I wouldn't be raped again.

Don't feel weak or get down on yourself if you need help. If you find yourself in this state of mind, ask yourself if you would treat a friend who had been raped just as harshly. If the answer is no, ask yourself why you won't treat yourself with the same compassion. Try to give yourself more credit. For example, many rape survivors have trouble sleeping immediately after the assault. If you are experiencing this problem, don't feel weak if you want to take medicinal sleeping aids. Of course, you want to be careful about chemical dependency, but everyone needs sleep. Immediately following an assault, one of the things you need most is some rest and peace. Just be careful not to depend on the pills for an extended period of time or use them to numb your feelings.

REMEMBERING

After an initial feeling of control is regained, you can begin to remember and reconstruct the assault so that it becomes part of your life story in a way that is psychologically acceptable. In a nutshell, you have to go through the muck to reach dry land. You can't make peace with yourself until you express and understand your feelings. As Freud writes, "the [patient] must find the courage to direct his attention to the phenomena of his illness. His illness must no longer seem to him contemptible, but must become an enemy worthy of his mettle, a piece of his personality, which has solid ground for existence, and out of which things of value for his future life have to be derived."*

This can be a difficult part of the recovery process. Why would anyone want to purposely expose herself to pain and anger when the initial impact of the assault is just becoming bearable? The assault is an experience you have had, and it is part of who you are. Denying its effect in the long term will only magnify and entrench its power over you. Often the first step is just telling the story of the assault. When you do this, whether to yourself or to others, you are asking these people to bear witness to your experience. Once you get the courage to share your experience, it might be hard to stop.

Some rape survivors may do this, even when it makes others uncomfortable, because the issues they are dealing with may always be present. Their feelings can be overwhelmingly powerful, and bottling them up can feel terrible. In addition, surviving a rape can rock the core assumptions of your identity. As you try to make sense of your emotional state in the aftermath, you can feel like a different person. It's only natural for you to want to share this new identity with others— especially since a common recovery response is to be intolerant of any perceived superficiality or deceit in yourself and/or others. When you take all these factors into consideration, it's easier to see why some rape survivors go through a phase when talking about their rape is almost an obsession. It is hoped, as time passes, that other, more positive experiences will take their place alongside the rape.

When you remember and acknowledge the pain of your assault, it is natural to grieve. You may think that a part of you died during the attack. Grieving is not an act of weakness; it is an act of courage. You do not give anything to your

---

* Freud, *Remembering, Repeating, and Working Through*, vol. 12, trans. J. Strachey (London: Hogarth Press, 1958), p. 145.

attacker by allowing yourself to grieve. It takes a tremendous amount of courage to face these feelings. You should be proud that you are able to recognize them, not humiliated because you feel weak. Because the process requires a great deal of introspection, it is possible to discover which of your characteristics you value and which ones you would like to change or shed.

As you remember, your feelings may also cause you to fantasize about exacting revenge on the assailant. In some ways, revenge fantasies can be an attempt to master or control the pain you feel, but they won't undo the harm done to you. Taking revenge in real life dehumanizes you and doesn't help to reconcile your anger. A rape survivor remembers:

> I would fantasize about hurting him in very humiliating ways, and he would be powerless to stop whatever I wanted to do to him. I could punch, kick, and slap him, and he was helpless. Sometimes I would get so wrapped up in revenge that it was hard for me to concentrate on anything else.

No matter how you look at it, unless you are defending yourself against a physical attack, it's wrong to hurt another human being.

RECONNECTION AND INTEGRATION

After surviving a rape, one of the most common reactions is to feel lonelier than you could ever have imagined. Feeling cut off from the rest of the human race can be devastating. The third phase of the recovery process seeks to resolve this isolation as the rape survivor reconnects with the relationships and environments that she has felt removed from. This means doing things that can be very difficult: trusting people, trusting yourself, and trying to live a life of awareness, not of fear. It means trusting yourself to know when to trust other people and situations, and when not to. During this phase, it is possible to realize that you have relationships with people you can't trust. Anne remarked that after her rape she went through a period of reevaluating her relationships:

> After the rape, the world as I knew it became very small. I made the choice to let go of certain friendships that were unhealthy for me. It was difficult to do because often these were friends I cared deeply about. But I felt that they could not be there for me.
>
> One friend's feelings were particularly harmful to me. She believes that most date and acquaintance rapes occur at the point when sexual intercourse is about to take place. The woman decides against it in order to tease the man she is with. My friend believes that in this instance the woman should not be surprised if she is raped and should take responsibility for it.
>
> I think she believes it is the woman's responsibility because this allows her to feel in control. By placing the blame on the woman, she is giving herself a false sense of security. If she put the responsibility of the rape where it really belongs, with the rapist, she would have to admit that she could be raped as well.

If you do not come to terms with the challenges of being close to people, there is a possibility that your future relationships will be shaped by the remnants of your isolation, and this will manifest itself in a prolonged reluctance to share yourself intimately with others. Then the rape will have succeeded in denying you one of the great rewards of being a human being—the capacity to love.

SEXUALITY AND INTIMACY

Sexual intimacy can be a difficult challenge during this phase. You have experienced an assault that can easily destroy your desire to be emotionally and/or physically close with another person, and the relationship doesn't have to be sexual for you to feel uncomfortable. Give yourself time to become comfortable; make sure that you feel in control of your body and that your wishes will be respected. It is critical that you have a supportive and respectful partner. But no matter what, being comfortable in a sexually intimate environment can be extremely difficult, even if both partners try their best to be patient and sensitive. Christina describes her experience:

> I think the last stage of my own healing is dealing with sexual intercourse and intimacy. I have a hard time believing that when I lie in someone's arms he will not do anything to hurt me. I can never relax. Casual sex is out of the question.

Another rape survivor says:

> Intimacy is difficult, uncomfortable, and new. Humiliation, rejection, and loss now feel natural. I am so frightened that I will get hurt, I don't let guys get close to me physically or emotionally. After three years, I am just beginning to feel more comfortable around them. Patience, trial and error, trust, and humor are key in relationships, especially sexual ones.

It is important to give yourself some time to become more comfortable with sexual intimacy. You may feel comfortable a week after the assault, or you may be uncomfortable a year later. You may also feel comfortable being intimate with someone one week, and then the next week you can't stand anyone being near you. The key is to take it a step at a time and to stop whenever you feel out of control. That may mean becoming comfortable speaking with someone about your feelings, holding someone's hand, or, when you are ready, hugging. If your partner unintentionally does something that makes you feel vulnerable, tell him or her. Don't assume someone can read your mind or be able to figure out what bothers you. Remember how great it can feel to be touched. Catie remembers how she was able to have her first relationship after the rape: "He wanted to gain my trust, and sex was not an issue. I didn't have to worry about him taking something from me, so I felt as though I could trust him."

FLASHBACKS AND NIGHTMARES

During any of the recovery phases it is natural for your mind to respond to the trauma by having a flashback or nightmare. A flashback is an intrusive image that brings the survivor back to the scene of the attack. It can come in the form of vivid pictures, sights, sounds, and smells. A flashback can occur at any time for any reason. It can literally stop you in your tracks.

> I was trying on a dress in a large department store in a small fitting room. I guess the size of the room reminded me of the room I was raped in, but the next moment I could see and feel it happening again. I almost felt as if he were there, forcing his penis in and out of me. I ran out of the fitting room to the ladies' room and vomited. After a few minutes I began to relax and could feel my sense of reality coming back to me.

Another common reaction to an assault is nightmares. Nightmares are a coping mechanism; they are a way for your body to recount the assault in a controlled, safe, and protected environment. Often survivors experience a nightmare with a repetitive theme or a replay of the assault itself. One rape survivor describes her repetitive dream:

My dreams are not exactly frightening; they are more frustrating. Even though years have passed since the rape, I still have them sometimes. Basically, in the dreams I can be in different environments, but I am always trying to convince the rapist to listen to me. When I try to explain what I want, he leaves, or I suddenly can't find him. During the rest of the dream I try to find him and become increasingly frustrated.

Do not ignore nightmares; people have them for a purpose. Repetitive nightmares can be an attempt to gain mastery and control over your feelings about the assault. They can desensitize you so that you can reach a place where you are more comfortable confronting your feelings. Unfortunately, nightmares can be emotionally disturbing and can make it difficult to return to sleep. People have different ways of dealing with this. Some think of a situation, place, or person to create a feeling of security and peace. Others try to go back over the nightmare to decipher its meaning. (If you can understand why you are afraid, often the fear will decrease.) Still others purposely try to have the nightmare again but change the ending to a more favorable one while awake, and then try to make that change in the nightmare. It takes a brave soul to attempt this. But counselors I have spoken with have frequently said that they have had clients who were able to create nightmares with more positive outcomes.

In both nightmares and flashbacks it is important to be able to ground yourself in reality after the event is over. In some cases, it is possible to stop flashbacks from occurring by reassuring yourself of your present state and the surrounding environment. One coping strategy is to tune in to your physical senses. Make a concerted effort to look at something, hear a sound, feel an object, or smell an odor that grounds you in the present. Some people regain their sense of reality by having an object on their body at all times that symbolizes the present. For example, if you wear a watch all the time, use it to symbolize the present: make it root you in the here and now. When you feel lost, look at the watch to bring you back. Another coping strategy is to learn relaxing and breathing exercises. One that I do is to concentrate on warming my hands and feet by breathing slowly and visualizing my hands and feet near a fire in a fireplace.

Nightmares and flashbacks can make you feel as though you are not making any progress after the attack. It can be very frustrating when, years later, you experience feelings that make you doubt you will ever be free of its powerful clutches. Instead of regarding them as setbacks, see them as part of a recovery process where you are constantly adapting to your fears with new coping mechanisms. As your recovery progresses, you will react with new insights and awareness.

FAMILY AND LOVED ONES

A rape is difficult not only for the survivor but also for family and friends. They can easily feel helpless when confronted with your pain and anger. Often people want to protect the survivor from any more suffering, so they try to make things as easy as possible. As every survivor responds uniquely to an assault, so do family and friends. Some are supportive, loving, and willing to go through a long and sometimes frustrating process as the survivor tries to regain control of her life. Unfortunately, there are families that are not supportive. And even in the best families, a crisis of this magnitude can bring out and/or exacerbate family tensions. Each situation has its challenges. In a loving family, you must make sure that your family does not become overprotective and prevent the recovery process from being your own. Because no matter how much family support you have, recovery after an assault is an individual process. As a survivor, you must also guard against hiding your pain or worrying about your loved one's pain more than your own.

If a family member is not supportive, you must evaluate your relationship and decide if it is in your best interest to continue it. Are there some positive elements in the relationship? If so, what are they? Is there a way to continue the relationship without allowing this person's feelings about your experience to affect your self-esteem or self-worth? If the relationship is one where the two of you can separate your feelings about the assault from the rest of your interaction, then you may want to continue it. If not, seriously consider suspending the relationship until you feel that this person will no longer negatively affect your recovery process. A rape survivor explains her feelings:

> I resent some members of my family, because when they were having hard times I was there for them. Then when I needed help, they wouldn't give it. It was difficult for my family to see the way I changed after the rape. I refused to go back to my old role, where I used to do all these things for other people. After the rape I didn't want to give like that anymore. I think it frightened them to see me fall apart and then pick myself up as a totally different person.

No matter what relationship you have with your family, their biggest challenge is accepting the choices you make. They may not like those choices, but it's not their life. You have to do whatever you think is best for you and for no one else.

GETTING PROFESSIONAL HELP

For most people who have survived a sexual assault, some kind of counseling can expedite the recovery process. Good therapists perceive themselves as their patients' allies and assistants in a shared journey of psychological healing. This is not to say that everyone must have counseling to put the pieces back together.

One of the benefits of therapy is that someone with professional expertise can be a good guide as you struggle along the recovery path. As I have said before, it is easy to feel incredibly lonely after an assault, and a therapist can help you explain and understand your feelings of isolation. A professional has a more objective viewpoint and can point out some options you may not be able to see because you are too close to your pain. For example, you may be suffering from recurrent nightmares for months or years after the rape that prohibit you from sleeping and leave you in a deeply anxious state. You may not know what to do. Some people attempt to numb their feelings by taking drugs or alcohol. With a counselor you can address the root causes of the nightmares and develop alternative strategies to face these feelings and to help you sleep without depending on chemical assistance.

How do you pick a good therapist? You can call the sexual-assault center near you and ask what services they have or if they have a referral service. You can also call professional associations (look them up in the white pages of your telephone directory, or call information) that represent counselors, social workers, and psychologists, and ask them for a list of professionals located in your area. Clinical social workers, psychologists, and psychiatrists are all professionals who can help. More important than the professional's title or degree is his/her experience and knowledge of sexual assault and recovery. Some therapists can be great therapists, but they might not feel comfortable discussing rape or other kinds of sexual and physical assault.

When you look for a therapist, think of yourself as a buyer. You are shopping for the best service possible. Interview potential therapists. Before you see them, call and explain that you are looking for a therapist and would like to meet with them. Ask about their fees, and check your medical insurance to see if any of the counseling expenses are covered. If you are on a limited budget, ask them if they have a sliding scale or payment plans. If they work through a county program, they probably will have both. Do not be intimidated because they are professionals. Ask about their experience with sexual-assault survivors. How many rape survivors have they worked with and for how long? Their job is to assist you in your healing process. Choosing a therapist is your decision. Trust your gut feeling. If you feel comfortable with the therapist, it's very possible s/he would be a good choice.

Should you choose a male or a female therapist? Does it make a difference? Yes and no. I don't think it follows that women are always better therapists than men for treating rape survivors. As in any profession, it primarily depends on the individual. There are male therapists who are very effective in counseling rape survivors, and there are female therapists who are not. However, I do think that effective female therapists can have better insight into the recovery process, because they know through personal experience what it feels like to live in a woman's body. Christina comments:

I felt as though a female therapist was needed for me at a certain point in my therapy, because I personally could not grow any further with my male therapist. There were certain things that I could not discuss comfortably with him . . . After the rape I felt as though I had no gender. Because my new therapist was feminine, assertive, and strong, she made me feel that it was okay to be a woman and to be strong. I never saw her outside the office, but she was willing to give me some personal insights. She helped me by setting an example.

You reach a time in your recovery process where therapy is no longer necessary. But how do you know when you have reached this point? It should be a mutual decision between you and your therapist. It can be a difficult decision, because you have worked hard together and you don't want to let go of the relationship. You may also feel dependent on the relationship; how are you going to face future problems on your own? Again, a rape survivor explains it best: "I can deal with daily problems on my own. Basically I go to therapy now for reassurance. It is difficult to end because I have been in therapy for four years. But I realize that in order to grow anymore I will need to let go." You may need to return to therapy to deal with issues that come up later, but don't think you have failed if you need to go back.

Another way of processing your feelings about the assault is to take a good self-defense class. In conjunction with therapy, I believe it is an excellent method of exploring and dealing with the issues surrounding a sexual assault. It is also an effective and safe way to express your anger without endangering yourself. In our self-defense classes, you can be presented with a situation like the one you experienced, face the fear, and fight through it. A rape survivor describes her feelings in class:

> So there I was waiting to be attacked. It's a frightening feeling, even knowing that you won't be hurt. I walked by him, trying to be cool, but shaking all over, sure that I wouldn't remember a single thing . . . I got in a few kicks . . . and then I realized he was on the ground. And a weird thing happened: I felt good about it. I suddenly felt that standing up for myself was a distinct possibility. That is an amazing feeling.

The biggest challenge I have faced as an instructor is allowing my students to go through fear, rage, and doubt as they learn self-defense. I want them to bypass all those bad things and get straight to the good stuff—the pride and joy they feel after having faced their fears and overcome them. At one point, I went to a therapist for help and guidance. She said to me, "Is it possible that you feel this way because you don't want anyone to go through what you did? You have to let them get through it on their own. Let them express their feelings, so they can face their fears and vanquish them."

I think of the recovery process in the same way. It is a painful experience, yet sometimes it offers you the chance to truly know yourself. And in the end, it is worth going through the pain to get to a point where you come to terms with the rape. For anyone going through this process, don't give up. All of the women I have spoken with about recovering from a rape seem to come out of it with resilience and power. These women are strong. Join them by knowing your quality of life is worth struggling for, and demand a safer, better future for yourself and all women.

To the Advocate, Family, or Significant Other

If you are reading this book because someone you care about is recovering from an assault, you need some strategies to get through this process, too. You could be torn by many conflicting emotions: anger, sorrow, grief, and/or disbelief. In the midst of these feelings, someone you love has been deeply hurt and is in pain. How can you be most helpful to her?

Remember, there is no way to predict how long it will take her to reach the reconnection and integration phase. So try not to have expectations about the time she needs to get back to normal. She may never feel like the person she was before the rape, or she may feel fine after a few weeks. Barbara survived a rape in her home, which occurred when her husband was out of town.

> For a while my husband felt guilty because he was not at home. But I never blamed him and felt better after about two weeks. We talked about our feelings and I felt that I was able to pretty quickly separate the rape from the rest of my life. After the initial shock and pain subsided, I wanted to concentrate on the good things in my life.

The most helpful thing you can do is let the survivor do what she feels is necessary for her recovery. And stand by her every step of the way.

Your biggest challenge is twofold: being there for her while not protecting her from her own pain, and taking care of yourself. Her recovery process may be a long one, and it can be exhausting for both of you. She may question every relationship she has, including the one she has with you. If this is the case, be patient. Don't force her to realize that you are the "good guy." She needs to make her own decisions, and her choices should be respected. A rape survivor's boyfriend describes his experience in the beginning of their relationship:

> At first it was hard because she was so emotionally closed and frightened. I think one of the critical factors is being patient and consistent, and convincing her that you can be trusted. If you think this person is worth it, you have to be patient until she feels comfortable.

Try to establish some parameters together. When doing so, remember that it is important to your emotional health as individuals and to the health of your relationship that you talk about the feelings you have—even if those feelings include anger or resentment toward the other person. If you have negative feelings, it's more effective to say, "I feel x," instead of, "You make me feel x." That way the person you are speaking with does not become defensive.

It is also important for the significant other to establish time-out periods or boundaries. It's natural to become overwhelmed by the pain, sadness, and anger of someone you love. You can become depressed or emotionally exhausted. It's also easy to go through a period of resentment, because you may be ready to move past the pain of the rape while she is not. A rape survivor can go through a time where she needs a tremendous amount of emotional support, and sometimes she can't give a lot back. Even though you are trying to help her, she may have difficulty trusting you. Another boyfriend of a rape survivor explains:

> Sometimes it's hard, because I haven't done anything wrong and she still doesn't trust me. I have thought to myself, "Why is she lumping me in the same category with this other guy?"

She is going through a time when getting her life back together, however that may be, is the most important thing she has to do. She may not be able to trust you and may be able to focus only on herself. So you or your feelings might not seem important during this time. It is critical to your ability to support her and to your emotional health that you have someone you can talk to and that you take time away from helping her in order to take care of yourself.

Immediately after the rape (usually the first three months), allow her to get over the initial shock and pain however she wants, even if that includes calling you or waking you up at three in the morning. But at a mutually agreeable point in time, you should establish boundaries for her dependence on you. For example, if she has a nightmare and wakes up at three in the morning, agree beforehand that she try to wait until seven to call you. And if she is doing strange things— such as checking the closets and under the beds—or is acting paranoid, let her do so as many times as she needs. You can even think of exercises to do together to make her more comfortable. For example, you can check the closets and she can look under the beds. Or, you can check out the house together.

No matter how supportive or wonderful you are, you will not be able to "fix" her pain for her. It's going to be difficult to see someone you love going through this kind of recovery. She has to do it herself. You can't do it for her, but you can be by her side as she goes through the process.

APPENDIX I
SEXUAL-ASSAULT CRISIS CENTERS IN THE UNITED STATES

Note: TDD indicates services for the hearing impaired.

National Resource Center on Domestic Violence: (800) 537-2238

ALABAMA

Birmingham
Rape Response Program
3600 Eighth Ave. South
Birmingham, AL 36302
Hot Line / Office: (205) 323-7273

Dothan
Wiregrass Comprehensive Mental Health Center
104 Prevatt Rd.
P.O. Drawer 1245
Dothan, AL 36302
Hot Line: (205) 794-0300
Office: (205) 712-2141

Montgomery
Council Against Rape
830 S. Court St.
Montgomery, AL 36104
Hot Line: (205) 286-5980
Office: (205) 286-5987

ALASKA

Anchorage
Standing Together Against Rape
111 E. Thirteenth St.
Anchorage, AK 99510
Hot Line / Office: (907) 276-7273

Fairbanks
Women in Crisis—Counseling and Assistance, Inc.
702 Tenth Ave.
Fairbanks, AK 99701
Hot Line: (907) 452-7273
Office: (907) 452-2293

Kenai
Lee Shore Rape Intervention
    Program
Women's Resource Center
325 Spruce St.
Kenai, AK 99611
Hot Line / Office: (907) 283-9479

Nome
Bering Sea Women's Group
P.O. Box 1596
Nome, AK 99762
Office: (907) 443-5444
Hot Line: (800) 570-5444

ARIZONA

Mesa
Center Against Sexual Abuse
    (CASA)
225 East 1st Street, Suite 109
Mesa, AZ 85201
Hot Line: (602) 241-9010
Office: (602) 898-8915

Prehab of Arizona
Autumn House Domestic Violence
    Shelter
P.O. Drawer 5860
Mesa, AZ 85201
Hot Line / Office: (602) 969-4024
Fax: (602) 969-0039

Phoenix
Rape Assault Crisis Center
5227 North 7th St., Suite 109
Phoenix, AZ 85014
Hot Line: (602) 241-9010
Office: (602) 241-9443

Scottsdale
Center Against Sexual Abuse
    (CASA)
7700 East Roosevelt
Scottsdale, AZ 85257
Hot Line: (602) 241-9010
Office: (602) 241-9443

Tempe
Center Against Sexual Abuse
    (CASA)
3030 South Rural Rd., Suite 101
Tempe, AZ 85282
Hot Line: (602) 241-9010
Office: (602) 898-8195

ARKANSAS

Fort Smith
Rape Crisis Inc.
401 Lexington Ave.
Fort Smith, AR 72901
Hot Line / Office: (501) 663-3334

Little Rock
Rape Crisis, Inc.
7509 Cantrell #211
Little Rock, AR 72207
Hot Line / Office: (501) 663-3334

CALIFORNIA

Berkeley
Bay Area Women Against Rape
1515 Webster Avenue
Oakland, CA 94612
Hot Line: (510) 845-7273
Office: (510) 465-3890

Chico
Rape Crisis Intervention of North
  Central California
P.O. Box 423
Chico, CA 95927
Hot Line / Office: (916) 891-1331

Claremont
Project Sister Rape Crisis Service
520 N. Indian Hill Blvd.
Claremont, CA 94523
Hot Line / Office: (909) 626-4357

Concord
Rape Crisis Service of Concord
1760 Clayton Rd.
Concord, CA 94523
Hot Line: (510) 798-RAPE
Office: (510) 237-0113

Davis
Yolo County Sexual Assault
  Center
222 D St.
Davis, CA 95616
Woodland Hotline: (916) 758-8400
E. Yolo Hotline: (916) 371-1907
Woodland Office: (916) 661-6636
E. Yolo Office: (916) 661-6336

Fairfield
Upper Solano Rape Crisis Service
P.O. Box 368
Fairfield, CA 94533
Hot Line / Office: (707) 422-RAPE
Hot Line / Office: (707) 644-RAPE

Fort Bragg
Community Assistance in Assault
  and Rape Emergency (CAARE
  Project, Inc.)
461 N. Franklin St.
Fort Bragg, CA 95437
Hot Line / Office: (707) 964-4357

Fresno
Rape Counseling Service of
  Fresno, Inc.
1060 Fulton Mall, Suite 901
Fresno, CA 93721
Hot Line: (209) 222-7273
Office: (209) 497-2900

Laguna Beach
Rape Crisis Unit
Laguna Beach Free Clinic
460 Ocean Ave.
Laguna Beach, CA 92651
Hot Line / Office: (714) 494-0761

Lompoc
Lompoc Rape Crisis Center
P.O. Box 148
Lompoc, CA 93438
Hot Line / Office: (805) 736-7273

Los Angeles
Los Angeles Commission on Assaults Against Women
6043 Hollywood Blvd., Suite 200
Los Angeles, CA 90028
Hot Line / Office: (213) 462-1281
Hot Line / Office: (213) 462-1356-
Self-defense
Fax: (213) 462-8434
Hot Line / Office: (310) 392-8381-
L.A. County
Hot Line / Office: (213) 626-3393-
Central Los Angeles
TDD: (213) 462-8410

Long Beach
Long Beach Rape Hotline
P.O. Box 14377
Long Beach, CA 90803
Hot Line / Office: (310) 597-2002

Monterey
Rape Crisis of the Monterey
  Peninsula
P.O. Box 2630
Monterey, CA 93942
Hot Line: (408) 633-5900
Office: (408) 633-2953

Orange
Orange County Rape Crisis
  Hotline
1107 E. Chapman
Orange, CA 92666
Hot Line: (714) 831-9110
Office: (714) 834-4317

Palo Alto
Mid-Peninsula Rape Crisis Center
  at the YWCA
4161 Alma St.
Palo Alto, CA 94306
Hot Line: (415) 493-RAPE
Office: (415) 494-0972

Pasadena
Rape Hotline Exchange
Pasadena–Foothill Valley YWCA
78 N. Marengo Ave.
Pasadena, CA 91101
Hot Line: (818) 793-3385
Office: (818) 793-5171

Placentia
Alpha Center
117 N. Main St.
Placentia, CA 92670
Hot Line: (714) 993-4400
Office: (714) 993-4403

Riverside
Riverside Area Rape Crisis Center
1465 Spruce St., Suite G
Riverside, CA 92507
Hot Line / Office: (909) 686-7273
Fax: (909) 686-0839

San Bernardino
San Bernardino Rape Crisis Intervention Service
1875 N. D St.
San Bernardino, CA 92405
Hot Line: (800) 222-RAPE
Hot Line: (909) 882-5291
Office: (909) 883-8689

San Diego
Center for Women's Services and
Studies
2467 E St.
San Diego, CA 92101
Hot Line: (619) 233-3088
Office: (619) 233-8984

San Francisco
San Francisco Women Against
Rape
3543 Eighteenth St.
San Francisco, CA 94110
Hot Line / Office: (415) 647-RAPE

San Jose
YWCA
375 S. Third St.
San Jose, CA 95112
Hot Line: (408) 287-3000
Office: (408) 295-4011

San Luis Rey
Women's Resource Center
4070 Mission Ave.
San Luis Rey, CA 92068
Hot Line / Office: (619) 757-3500

San Pablo
Rape Crisis Center of West Contra
Costa
c/o Brookside Hospital
Vale Rd.
San Pablo, CA 94806
Hot Line / Office: (415) 236-7273

San Rafael
Marin Rape Crisis Center
P.O. Box 392
San Rafael, CA 94902
Hot Line / Office: (415) 924-2100

Santa Ana
Sexual Assault Victims Services /
Prevention Program
Superior Court, County of Orange
700 Civic Center Dr. West
Santa Ana, CA 92701
Hot Line: (714) 957-2737
Office: (714) 834-4317

Santa Barbara
Santa Barbara Rape Crisis Center
111 N. Milpas St.
Santa Barbara, CA 93103
Hot Line: (805) 569-2255
Office: (805) 963-6832

Santa Cruz
Defensa de Mujeres
1215 Mission St.
Santa Cruz, CA 95060
Hot Line / Office: (408) 426-7273

Santa Maria
North County Rape Crisis and
Child Protection Center
P.O. Box 6202
Santa Maria, CA 93456
Hot Line: (805) 928-3554
Office: (805) 922-2994

Santa Monica
Rape Treatment Center
Santa Monica Hospital Medical
Center
1225 Fifteenth St.
Santa Monica, CA 90404
Office: (310) 319-4000

Santa Rosa
Sonoma County Women Against
  Rape
P.O. Box 1426
Santa Rosa, CA 95402
Hot Line: (707) 545-7273
Office: (707) 545-7270

Stockton
Sexual Assault Center of San Joa-
  quin County
930 N. Commerce
Stockton, CA 95202
Hot Line: (209) 465-4997
Office: (209) 941-2611

Watsonville
Defensa de Mujeres
406 Main St. #326
Watsonville, CA 95076
Hot Line: (408) 685-3737
Office: (408) 722-4532

COLORADO

Boulder
Mental Health Center
Attn: Ronah Brodkin
Rape Crisis Team
1333 Iris Street
Boulder, CO 80302
Hot Line / Office: (303) 443-7300

Denver
Rape Crisis Center
P.O. Box 18951
Denver, CO 80218-0951
Hot Line: (303) 322-7273
Office: (303) 329-9922

Grand Junction
Rape Crisis Center
1129 Colorado Ave.
Grand Junction, CO 81501
Hot Line / Office: (303) 243-0190

Greenley
Weld County Sexual Assault Sup-
  port Team
Box 240
Greenley, CO 80632
Hot Line / Office: (303) 362-RAPE

CONNECTICUT

Bridgeport
Rape Crisis Service / YWCA
753 Fairfield Ave.
Bridgeport, CT 06604
Hot Line: (203) 333-2233
Office: (203) 525-1163

Hartford
Sexual Assault Crisis Service
YWCA
135 Broad St.
Hartford, CT 06105
Hot Line: (203) 522-6666
Office: (203) 334-6154, ext. 240

Middletown
SAFE, Middlesex County Sexual
  Assault Crisis Service
Community Health Center
P.O. Box 1514
Middletown, CT 06457
Hot Line / Office: (203) 364-7233

Milford
Milford Rape Crisis Center
70 West River St.
Milford, CT 06460-3317
Hot Line / Office: (203) 878-1212

New Haven
New Haven YWCA
Rape Crisis Center
48 Howe St.
New Haven, CT 06511
Hot Line / Office: (203) 624-2273

New London
Women's Center Rape Crisis
  Service
16 Jay St.
New London, CT 06320
Hot Line: (203) 442-4357
Office: (203) 447-0366

Stamford
Rape Crisis Service of Stamford
c/o Stamford Hospital
Shelburn Rd.
Stamford, CT 06901
Hot Line: (203) 329-2929
Office: (203) 348-9346

Waterbury
Waterbury YWCA
Sexual Assault Crisis Service of
  the Central Naugatuck Valley,
  Inc.
80 Prospect St.
Waterbury, CT 06702
Hot Line / Office: (203) 753-3613

DELAWARE

Milford
CONTACT Delaware
P.O. Box 61
Milford, DE 19963
Hot Line: (800) 262-9800
Office: (302) 422-2078

Wilmington
CONTACT Delaware
P.O. Box 9525
Wilmington, DE 19809
Hot Line: (302) 761-9100
Fax: (302) 761-4280

Crisis House
110 North Railroad Ave.
Wilmington, DE 19809
Hot Line / Office: (302) 856-2246

DISTRICT OF COLUMBIA

Washington, D.C.
D.C. Rape Crisis Center
P.O. Box 215005
Washington, D.C. 20009
Hot Line / Office: (202) 232-0202

FLORIDA

Gainesville
Rape / Crime Victim Advocate
  Program
730 N. Waldo Rd., Building "B,"
  Suite 100
Gainesville, FL 32601
Hot Line: (904) 377-6888
Office: (904) 372-3659

Miami
Rape Treatment Center
1611 N.W. Twelfth Ave.
Miami, FL 33136
Hot Line: (305) 325-7273
Office: (305) 585-6469

Pensacola
Rape Crisis Center of West
  Florida
Lakeview Center
1221 W. Lakeview Ave.
Pensacola, FL 32501
Hot Line / Office: (904) 433-7273

Sarasota
SPARCC—Safe Place and Rape
  Crisis Center of Sarasota, Inc.
P.O. Box 1675
Sarasota, FL 33579
Hot Line: (813) 365-1976
Office: (813) 365-0208

Tampa
Hillsborough County Crisis Center
2214 E. Henry St.
Tampa, FL 33610-4479
Hot Line: (813) 228-RAPE
Office: (813) 238-8411
Fax: (813) 238-8300
TDD: (813) 238-8821

GEORGIA

Atlanta
Rape Crisis Center / Cobb County
  YWCA
438 Fraser St. S.E.
Atlanta, GA 31312
Hot Line / Office: (404) 428-2666

Savannah
Rape Crisis Center of the Coastal
  Empire, Inc.
P.O. Box 8492
Savannah, GA 31412
Hot Line: (912) 233-RAPE
Office: (912) 354-6742

HAWAII

Hilo
YWCA: Sexual Assault Support
  Service
145 Ululani St.
Hilo, HI 96720
Hot Line: (808) 935-0677
Office: (808) 935-7141

Honolulu
Sex Abuse Treatment Center
Kapiolani Children's Medical
  Center
1319 Punahoe St.
Honolulu, HI 96826
Hot Line: (808) 524-7273
Office: (808) 973-8337

Kailua-Kona
Kailua-Kona Rape Crisis Center
75-5759 Kuakini Hwy. #103C
Kailua-Kona, HI 96740
Hot Line: (808) 935-0677
Office: (808) 334-0308

IDAHO

Boise
Rape Crisis Center
720 Washington Street
Boise, ID 83702
Hot Line / Office: (208) 345-7273

Caldwell
Rape Crisis Center of Canyon
County
1717 Arlington South
Caldwell, ID 83605
Hot Line / Office: (208) 454-0101

Coeur d'Alene
Lutheran Social Services
2201 Government Way, Suite H
Coeur d'Alene, ID 83814
Hot Line / Office: (208) 667-1898

Moscow
Women's Center at the University
of Idaho
Moscow, ID 83844-1064
Hot Line: (208) 885-6616 (day)
Hot Line: (208) 882-4511 (night)
Fax: (208) 885-9494

Nampa
Mercy House
P.O. Box 558
Nampa, ID 83653
Hot Line: (208) 465-5011
Office: (208) 467-4130

Pocatello
Pocatello Women's Advocates
454 N. Garfield
Pocatello, ID 83204
Hot Line: (208) 235-2503
Office: (208) 232-0742

Twin Falls
Volunteers Against Violence, Inc.
P.O. Box 2444
Twin Falls, ID 83301
Hot Line / Office: (208) 733-0100

ILLINOIS

Aurora
Mutual Ground, Inc.
Sexual Assault Services
P.O. Box 843
Aurora, IL 60506
Hot Line: (708) 897-8383
Office: (708) 897-8009
Fax: (708) 897-8439

Belleville
Sexual Assault Victims' Care Unit
9400 Lebanon Rd.
Edgemont, IL 62203
Hot Line: (618) 397-0975
Youth/Teen Line: (618) 397-8707
Office: (618) 397-0968

Bloomington
Rape Crisis Center of Mid-Central
Illinois
838 West Oakland
Bloomington, IL 61701
Hot Line / Office: (309) 827-4005

Carbondale
Rape Action Committee Women's
Center
406 West Mill
Carbondale, IL 62901
Hot Line / Office: (309) 529-2324

Charleston / Mattoon
Sexual Assault Counseling and In-
formation Service (SACIS)
2505 Kari Knoll
Charleston, IL 61920
Hot Line / Office: (217) 348-5033

Chicago

Chicago Women Against Rape
Loop YWCA—Women's Services
180 N. Wabash
Chicago, IL 60601
Hot Line: (312) 372-4105
Office: (312) 372-6600, ext. 239
Fax: (312) 372-4673

City of Chicago Department of Human Services
500 N. Prestigo Ct.
Chicago, IL 60611
Rape-Victim Hot Line: (312) 744-8418
Battered-Women Hot Line: (312) 744-6644

Community Counseling Centers of Chicago
Quetzal Center
5710 North Broadway
Chicago, IL 60660
Hot Line / Office: (312) 334-8608

Community Mental Health Council
8704 S. Constance Ave.
Chicago, IL 60617
Hot Line / Office: (312) 734-4033
Fax: (312) 734-5994

Family Violence Program
Rush Presbyterian St. Luke's Medical Center
1653 W. Congress Parkway
Chicago, IL 60612
Hot Line / Office: (312) 94-ABUSE

Harris YWCA Service to Rape Victims
6200 South Drexel
Chicago, IL 60637
Hot Line / Office: (312) 955-3100

Rape Victim Advocates
222 South Morgan, Suite 2C
Chicago, IL 60607
Hot Line / Office: (312) 733-6954

Collinsville

Sexual Assault Victims First
1600 Golf View, Suite 270
Collinsville, IL 62234
Hot Line: (618) 344-0605
Office: (618) 344-0609

Danville

YWCA Sexual Assault Crisis Services
201 North Hazel
Danville, IL 61832
Hot Line: (217) 443-5566
Office: (217) 446-1217

Decatur

Growing Strong: Sexual Assault Center
P.O. Box 45
Decatur, IL 62525
Hot Line / Office: (217) 428-0770

East St. Louis

Volunteers of America
4700 State St., Suite 2
East St. Louis, IL 62205
Hot Line / Office: (618) 271-9833

Edwardsville
Rape and Sexual Abuse Care
    Center
Southern Illinois University at
    Edwardsville
P.O. Box 154
Edwardsville, IL 62026-1154
Hot Line / Office: (618) 692-2197

Elgin
Community Crisis Center, Inc.
P.O. Box 1390
Elgin, IL 60121
Hot Line / Office: (708) 697-2380

Galena
Riverview Center
Sexual Assault Intervention and
    Prevention Services
P.O. Box 329
Galena, IL 61036
Hot Line / Office: (815) 777-8155

Glen Ellyn
YWCA of DuPage
YWCA West Suburban Area
739 Roosevelt Rd. #8, Suite 210
Glen Ellyn, IL 60137
Hot Line: (708) 971-3927
Office: (708) 790-6600

Gurnee
Lake County Council Against Sex-
    ual Assault
1 South Greenleaf St., Suite E
Gurnee, IL 60031
Hot Line: (708) 872-7799
Office: (708) 244-1187
Fax: (708) 244-6380

Joliet
Will County Rape Crisis Center
P.O. Box 2354
Joliet, IL 60434
Hot Line: (815) 722-3344
Office: (815) 744-5280

Kankakee
Kankakee County Center Against
    Sexual Assault
657 East Court St., Suite 220
Kankakee, IL 60901
Hot Line: (815) 932-3322
Office: (815) 932-7273
Fax: (815) 932-7298

Macomb
Western Illinois Regional Coun-
    cil—Community Action Agency
    Sexual Assault Program
223 South Randolph
Macomb, IL 61455
Hot Line: (309) 837-5555
Office: (309) 837-2997

Matteson
YW C.A.R.E.S.
South Suburban YWCA
4343 W. Lincoln Highway, Suite
    210
Matteson, IL 60443
Hot Line: (708) 748-5672
Office: (708) 748-6600
Fax: (708) 748-6606

Moline
Quad Cities Rape / Sexual Assault
Counseling Program
Family Resources, Inc.
111 19th Ave.
Moline, IL 61265
Hot Line: (309) 797-1777
Office: (309) 797-1888

Peoria
The Center for Prevention of
Abuse
P.O. Box 3172
Peoria, IL 61612-3172
Hot Line: (309) 691-4111
Hot Line: 800-559-SAFE
Office: (309) 691-0551 or 0552
Fax: (309) 691-0913

Quanada
2707 Maine St.
Quincy, IL 62301
Hot Line: (217) 22A-BUSE (222-
2873)
Hot Line: 800-369-2287
Office: (217) 222-3069

Quincy
Sexual Assault Prevention and In-
tervention Services (SAPIS)
510 Maine St.
WCU Building, Suite 600
Quincy, IL 62301
Hot Line: (217) 22A-BUSE
Hot Line: 800-369-2287
Office: (217) 223-2030
Fax: (217) 222-4574

Rockford
Rockford Sexual Assault Counsel-
ing, Inc.
202 W. State St., Suite 302
Rockford, IL 61101
Hot Line: (815) 964-2991
Office: (815) 962-4477

Schaumberg
Northwest Action Against Rape
870 East Higgins Rd., Suite 136
Schaumberg, IL 60173
Hot Line: (708) 228-0990
Office: (708) 517-4488

Springfield
Rape Information and Counseling
Service
110 West Laurel St.
Springfield, IL 62704
Hot Line: (217) 753-8081
Office: (217) 744-2560

Sterling
YWCA/COVE
412 First Ave.
Sterling, IL 61081-3697
Hot Line: (815) 626-7277
Office: (815) 625-0333

Summit
Des Plaines Valley Community
Center
6125 South Archer Road
Summit, IL 60501
Hot Line: (708) 482-9600
Office: (708) 458-6920

Urbana
A Woman's Fund, Inc. / Rape Crisis Services
505 West Green Street
Urbana, IL 61801
Hot Line: (217) 384-4444
Office: (217) 384-4462

Vandalia
Sexual Assault and Family Emergencies Corp.
P.O. Box 192
Vandalia, IL 62471
Hot Line / Office: (618) 283-1414

INDIANA

Fort Wayne
Rape Awareness
303 E. Washington Blvd.
Fort Wayne, IN 46802
(219) 426-7273

Lawrenceburg
Rape Crisis Intervention Team
Community Mental Health Center
285 Bielby Rd.
Lawrenceburg, IN 47025
Office: (812) 537-1302
Hot Line: (800) 832-5378

IOWA

Ames
Story County Sexual Assault Care Center
P.O. Box 1965, ISU Station
Ames, IA 50010
Hot Line / Office: (515) 232-2303

Cedar Rapids
Rape Crisis Services
YWCA
318 Fifth St. SE
Cedar Rapids, IA 52401
Hot Line: (319) 363-5490
Office: (319) 365-1458

Davenport
Quad Cities Rape / Sexual Assault Counseling Center of Scott and Rock Island Counties
P.O. Box 190
Davenport, IA 52805
Hot Line: (319) 326-9191
Office: (319) 797-1888

Des Moines
Iowa Coalition Against Sexual Assault (CASA)
Lucas State Office Building
Des Moines, IA 50319
Hot Line / Office: (515) 242-5096

Fort Dodge
Rape / Sexual Assault Victim Advocates
Trinity Regional Hospital
South Kenyon Rd.
Fort Dodge, IA 50501
Hot Line: (515) 573-8000
Office: (515) 955-2273

KANSAS

Atchison
DoVes
P.O. Box 262
Atchison, KS 66002
Hot Line: (913) 367-0363
Hot Line: 800-367-7075
Office: (913) 367-0365

Dodge City
Crisis Center of Dodge City
P.O. Box 1173
Dodge City, KS 67801
Hot Line: (316) 225-6987
Office: (316) 225-6510
Fax: (316) 227-3970

El Dorado
Family Life Center of Butler
  County
115 S. Washington, P.O. Box 735
El Dorado, KS 67042
Hot Line / Office: (316) 321-7104

Emporia
SOS, Inc.
P.O. Box 1191
Emporia, KS 66801
Hot Line: (316) 342-1870
Hot Line: (800) 825-1295

Garden City
Family Crisis Services
P.O. Box 1092
Garden City, KS 67846
Hot Line: (316) 275-2018
Office: (316) 275-5911

Great Bend
Family Crisis Center
P.O. Box 1543
Great Bend, KS 67530
Hot Line: (316) 792-3672
Office: (316) 792-1885

Hays
Northwest Kansas Family Shelter
P.O. Box 284
Hays, KS 67601
Hot Line: (913) 652-4202
Hot Line: (800) 794-4624

Horton
Native American Family Services,
  Inc.
(for Native Americans only)
P.O. Box 206
Horton, KS 66439
Hot Line / Office: (913) 4486-2837
Fax: (913) 486-2801

Northeast Kansas Family Violence
  Prevention Program
Route 1, Box 157-A
Horton, KS 66439
Hot Line: (800) 544-3167
Office: (913) 486-3591
Fax: (913) 486-2801

Humboldt
Rape Counseling
Southeast Kansas Mental Health
  Center
1106 S. Ninth St.
Humboldt, KS 66748
Hot Line / Office: (316) 473-2241

Hutchinson
Sexual Assault and Domestic Vio-
  lence Center of Reno County
1 E. 9th St.
Hutchinson, KS 67501-2856
Hot Line: (316) 633-2522
Office: (316) 665-3630

Women's Crisis Center (Rape
  Center)
Route 2, Box 37
Hutchinson, KS 67501
Hot Line: (316) 663-2522
Office: (316) 665-3630

Iola
Hope Unlimited
P.O. Box 12
Iola, KS 66749
(316) 365-4960

Junction City
Junction City—Geary County
  Rape Crisis Team
Geary County Hospital
Box 490
Junction City, KS 66441
Hot Line / Office: (913) 238-4131

Kansas City
Joyce Williams Haven
P.O. Box 172122
Kansas City, KS 66117
Hot Line / Office: (913) 995-1000
Fax: (913) 321-1569

Lawrence
Rape Victim / Survivor Service
  (RVSS)
1419 Massachusetts Ave.
Lawrence, KS 66044
Hot Line: (913) 841-2345
Office: (913) 843-8985

Women's Transitional Care
  Services
P.O. Box 633
Lawrence, KS 66044
Hot Line / Office: (913) 841-6887

Leavenworth
Alliance Against Family Violence
P.O. Box 465
Leavenworth, KS 66048
Hot Line: (913) 682-9131
Office: (913) 682-1752
Teen Talk Phone: (913) 682-3030

Liberal
Liberal Area Rape Crisis and Do-
  mestic Violence Service
150 Plaza Dr.
Liberal, KS 67901
Hot Line / Office: (316) 624-8818

Manhattan
Crisis Center, Inc.
P.O. Box 1526
Manhattan, KS 66044
(913) 539-2785

Mayetta
Native American Family Services,
  Inc.
P.O. Box 142
Mayetta, KS 66509
Hot Line / Office: (913) 966-2141

McPherson
McPherson County Council on Vi-
  olence Against Persons
514 N. Main St.
McPherson, KS 67460
Hot Line: (316) 241-7111
Office: (316) 241-6615

Morrill
Multi-County Domestic Violence
  Program, Inc.
Route 1, P.O. Box 199
Morrill, KS 66515
Hot Line: (913) 459-2859
Office: (913) 742-7125

Newton
Domestic Violence / Sexual Assault
  Association
P.O. Box 942
Newton, KS 67114
Hot Line: (800) 487-0510
Office: (316) 284-6920
Fax: (316) 284-6856

Overland Park
Safehome, Inc.
P.O. Box 4469
Overland Park, KS 66204
Hot Line: (913) 262-2868
Office: (913) 432-9300
Fax: (913) 432-9302

Pittsburg
Safehouse, Inc.
101 E. 4th, Suite 214 #10
Pittsburg, KS 66762
Hot Line: (800) 794-9148
Office: (316) 231-8692
Fax: (316) 231-8692

Salina
Domestic Violence Association of
  Central Kansas
1700 E. Iron
Salina, KS 67401
Hot Line: (800) 874-1499
Office: (913) 827-5862

Scott City
H.E.L.P.
P.O. Box 72
Scott City, KS 67871
Hot Line / Office: (316) 872-2420
Fax: (316) 872-7145

Topeka
YWCA
Battered Women's Task Force
  Sexual Assault Counseling
  Program
P.O. Box 1883
Topeka, KS 66601
Hot Line: (913) 233-1730
Office: (913) 354-7927
Fax: (913) 233-4867

Wichita
Wichita Area Sexual Assault Cen-
  ter, Inc.
215 N. St. Francis, Suite 1
Wichita, KS 67214
Hot Line: (316) 263-3002
Office: (316) 263-0185

Wichita Catholic Social Services
  Harbor House
P.O. Box 3759
Wichita, KS 67201-3759
Hot Line / Office: (316) 263-6000

YWCA Women's Crisis Center
P.O. Box 1740
Wichita, KS 67201
Hot Line: (316) 267-SAFE
Office: (316) 263-2313
Fax: (316) 264-1828

Winfield
Cowley County Safe Homes
P.O. Box 181
Winfield, KS 67156
Hot Line: (800) 794-7672 or (316)
  221-HELP
Office: (316) 221-7300

KENTUCKY

Covington
Women's Crisis Center
835 Madison Ave.
Covington, KY 41011
Hot Line / Office: (606) 491-3335

Florence
Women's Crisis Center
Boone County
11 Shelby St.
Florence, KY 41042
Hot Line / Office: (606) 525-2600

Lexington
Lexington Rape Crisis Center
P.O. Box 1603
Lexington, KY 40592
Hot Line: (316) 263-3002
Office: (316) 252-8514

Louisville
Center for Women and Families
P.O. Box 2048
Louisville, KY 40101-2048
Hot Line / Office: (502) 581-7273
Fax: (502) 581-7204

Maysville
Women's Crisis Center
111 East 3rd St.
P.O. Box 484
Maysville, KY 41056
Hot Line / Office: (606) 564-6708

Newport
Women's Crisis Center of Northern Kentucky
321 York St.
Newport, KY 41071
Hot Line / Office: (606) 491-3335

Owensboro
Rape Victims Services
2010 Triplett St.
Owensboro, KY 42303
Hot Line: (502) 926-RAPE
Hot Line: (800) 226-RAPE
Office: (502) 926-7278

Williamstown
Women's Crisis Center
205 North Main St.
P.O. Box 294
Williamstown, KY 41097
Hot Line / Office: (606) 824-7697

LOUISIANA

Alexandria
Work Against Rape
Sexual Assault Care Service / HELPLINE
1404 Murray St., P.O. Box 1908
Alexandria, LA 71309
Hot Line: (318) 445-2022
Office: (318) 448-0284

Baton Rouge
Stop Rape Crisis Center
East Baton Rouge Parish District
District Attorney's Office
233 St. Ferdinand St.
Baton Rouge, LA 70801
Hot Line / Office: (504) 383-RAPE

New Orleans
YWCA Rape Crisis Center
601 S. Jefferson Davis Pkwy.
New Orleans, LA 70119
Hot Line: (504) 483-8888
Office: (504) 482-9922

MAINE

Augusta
Augusta Area Rape Crisis Center
3 Mulliken Ct.
Augusta, ME 04330
Hot Line / Office: (207) 626-0660

Bangor
Rape Response Services
P.O. Box 2516
Bangor, ME 04401
Hot Line / Office: (800) 310-0000

Brunswick / Bath
Midcoast Sexual Assault Support
Center
P.O. Box 990
Brunswick, ME 04011
Hot Line / Office: (800) 822-5999

Ellsworth
Downeast Sexual Assault Services
P.O. Box 1087
Ellsworth, ME 04605
Hot Line / Office: (800) 228-2470

Farmington
S.A.V.E.S.
P.O. Box 349
Farmington, ME 04938
Hot Line / Office: (800) 221-9191

Auburn / Lewiston
Sexual Assault Crisis Center
P.O. Box 6
Auburn, ME 04212
Hot Line / Office: (800) 371-0000

Norway / South Paris
R.E.A.C.H.
17 Winter St.
Norway, ME 04268
Hot Line / Office: (800) 622-2365

Portland
The Rape Crisis Center, Inc.
P.O. Box 1371
Portland, ME 04104
Hot Line: (207) 774-3613
Office: (207) 799-9020

Presque Isle
Sexual Assault Helpline
162 Main St.
Presque Isle, ME 04769
Hot Line / Office: (800) 432-7805

Waterville
Rape Crisis Assistance
P.O. Box 924
Waterville, ME 04903-0924
Hot Line / Office: (800) 525-4441

MARYLAND

Annapolis
Anne Arundel County Sexual Assault Crisis Center
1127 West St.
Annapolis, MD 21401
Hot Line / Office: (301) 280-1321

Victim / Witness Assistance Center
101 South St.
Annapolis, MD 21401
Hot Line / Office: (301) 280-1160

Baltimore

House of Ruth
2201 Argonne Dr.
Baltimore, MD 21218
Hot Line: (301) 889-7884
Office: (301) 889-0840

Sexual Abuse Treatment Program
312 E. Oliver St.
Baltimore, MD 21202
Hot Line: (301) 361-2235
Office: (301) 361-3927

Sexual Assault Recovery Center
1010 St. Paul St.
Baltimore, MD 21202
Hot Line: (301) 366-RAPE
Office: (301) 685-0937

State's Attorney's Office for Balti-
more City—Sex Offense Unit
111 N. Calvert St., Courthouse
East, Room 316
Baltimore, MD 21202
Hot Line / Office: (301) 396-5040

Bel Air

Sexual Assault / Spouse Abuse Re-
source Center
101 Thomas St.
Bel Air, MD 21014
Hot Line: (301) 879-3486
Office: (301) 836-8430

Bethesda

Community Crisis Center / Sexual
Assault Services
4910 Auburn Ave.
Bethesda, MD 20814
Hot Line: (301) 656-9420
Office: (301) 656-9526

Sexology Associates, Inc.
4835 Del Ray Ave.
Bethesda, MD 20814-3013
Hot Line / Office: (301) 652-6448

California

Walden / Sierra, Inc.
P.O. Box 224
California, MD 20619
Hot Line: (301) 863-6661
Office: (301) 870-3646

Cheverly

Prince Georges County Sexual As-
sault Center
Prince Georges General Hospital
and Medical Center
3001 Hospital Dr.
Cheverly, MD 20785
Office: (301) 618-3154
Hospital: (301) 618-2000
After-Hours Hotline: (301) 618-
3162

MASSACHUSETTS

Amherst

Counselors / Advocates Against
Rape
Everywoman's Center, Wilder
Hall
University of Massachusetts
Amherst, MA 01003
Hot Line: (413) 545-0800
Office: (413) 545-0883

Boston
Rape Crisis Intervention Program
Beth Israel Hospital
330 Brookline Ave.
Boston, MA 02215
Office: (617) 735-4645

Cambridge
Boston Area Rape Crisis Center
Women's Center
46 Pleasant St.
Cambridge, MA 02026
Hot Line: (617) 492-RAPE
Office: (617) 492-8306

Dedham
Norfolk County Rape Unit
360 Washington St.
Dedham, MA 02026
Hot Line / Office: (617) 326-1111

MICHIGAN

Ann Arbor
Assault Crisis Center
2350 E. Stadium
Ann Arbor, MI 48104
Hot Line: (313) 944-2424
Office: (313) 994-2618

Detroit
Rape Counseling Center
Detroit Police Department
4201 St. Antoine
Detroit, MI 48201
Hot Line / Office: (313) 833-1660

East Lansing
Sexual Assault Counseling of the
  Listening Ear
547½ E. Grand River Ave.
East Lansing, MI 48823
Hot Line / Office: (517) 337-1717

Kalamazoo
Kalamazoo Sexual Assault
  Program
YWCA
353 East Michigan Ave.
Kalamazoo, MI 49007
Hot Line: (616) 345-3036
Office: (616) 345-9412

Muskegon
Rape / Spouse Assault Crisis Cen-
  ter of Every Woman's Place,
  Inc.
1433 Clinton
Muskegon, MI 49442
Hot Line: (616) 722-3333
Office: (616) 726-4493

Pontiac
Oakland Crisis Center for Rape
  and Sexual Abuse
YWCA of Pontiac–North Oakland
92 Whitmore St.
Pontiac, MI 48342
Hot Line: (313) 334-1274
Office: (313) 334-1284

Port Huron
St. Clair County Domestic Assault
and Rape Elimination Services
Task Force (DARES)
P.O. Box 610968
Port Huron, MI 48061-0968
Hot Line: (313) 985-5538
Office: (800) 985-4950

Saginaw
Saginaw County Sexual Assault
Center
1226 N. Michigan Ave.
Saginaw, MI 48602
Hot Line / Office: (517) 755-6565

MINNESOTA

Brainerd
Woman's Center of Mid-
Minnesota, Inc.
P.O. Box 602
Brainerd, MN 56401
Hot Line / Office: (218) 828-1216

Minneapolis
Rape and Sexual Assault Center
2431 Hennepin Ave. South
Minneapolis, MN 55405
Hot Line / Office: (612) 825-4357
(9:00 a.m.–7:30 p.m.)

Sexual Assault Resource Service at
Hennepin County Medical
Center
525 Portland Ave., Room 712
Minneapolis, MN 55415
Hot Line: (612) 347-3161
Office: (612) 347-5832

Sexual Violence Center
2100 Pillsbury Ave. South
Minneapolis, MN 55404
Hot Line: (612) 871-5111
Office: (612) 871-5100
Fax: (612) 871-1550

Rochester
Rapeline Program
151 4th St. S.E.
Rochester, MN 55904-3711
Hot Line / Office: (501) 289-0636

St. Cloud
Central Minnesota Sexual Assault
Center
601½ Mall Germain St. Suite 204
St. Cloud, MN 56301
Hot Line: (800) 273-5090
Office: (612) 251-4357

St. Paul
Sexual Offense Services of Ramsey
County (SOS)
1619 Dayton Ave.
St. Paul, MN 55104
Hot Line / Office: (612) 298-5898

Winona
Women's Resource Center
14 Exchange Bldg.
Winona, MN 55987
Hot Line / Office: (507) 452-4440

MISSOURI
Columbia
The Shelter
800 N. Providence, Suite 2
Columbia, MO 65201
Hot Line: (314) 875-1370
Office: (314) 875-1369

Kansas City
MOCSA
106 E. 31st Terr.
Kansas City, MO 64111
Hot Line: (816) 531-0233
Office: (816) 931-4527

Springfield
Rape Crisis Assistance, Inc.
943 Boonville
Springfield, MO 65802
Hot Line / Office: (417) 864-7273

MONTANA

Billings
Billings Rape Task Force
1245 N. Twenty-Ninth St., Room 218
Billings, MT 59101
Hot Line: (406) 259-6506
Office: (406) 245-6721

NEBRASKA

Auburn
Project Response
P.O. Box 213
Auburn, NE 68305
Hot Line: 800-456-5764
Office: (402) 274-5092
Counties served: Otoe, Johnson, Nemaha, Pawnee, Richardson

Bellevue
Family Service Domestic Abuse Program
116 E. Mission St.
Bellevue, NE 68005
Hot Line: (800) 523-3666 or (402) 444-4433
Office: (402) 291-6065
Counties served: Sarpy, Cass

Benkelman
Dundy County Task Force on Domestic Violence and Sexual Assault
P.O. Box 302
Benkelman, NE 69021
Hot Line: (308) 423-2676 or (800) 607-1497
Office: (308) 423-2498
Counties served: Dundy, Chase

Broken Bow
Domestic Abuse Crisis Center
425 S. 7th
Broken Bow, NE 68822
Hot Line: (800) 942-4040 or (308) 872-5988
Office: (308) 872-2420
Counties served: Custer, Blaine, Loup, Garfield, Wheeler, Valley, Greeley, Sherman

Columbus
Center for Sexual Assault and Domestic Violence Survivors
P.O. Box 42
Columbus, NE 68601
Hot Line: (402) 463-4677
Office: (402) 564-2155
Counties served: Boone, Nance, Platte, Colfax

Fairbury
Blue Valley Crisis Intervention
P.O. Box 273
Fairbury, NE 68352
Hot Line: (800) 777-7332
Office: (402) 729-2278
Counties served: Saunders, Butler,
    Polk, York, Fillmore, Saline,
    Seward, Thayer, Gage, Jefferson

Fremont
Domestic Abuse / Sexual Assault
    Crisis Center
P.O. Box 622
Fremont, NE 68025
Hot Line: (402) 727-7777 or (800)
    523-3666
Office: (402) 721-4340
Counties served: Dodge, Burt,
    Washington

Gordon
Family Rescue Services
107 E. 2nd St.
Gordon, NE 69343
Office: (308) 282-0126
Hot Line: (308) 432-4433 (in
    Chadron)
Counties served: Dawes, Sheridan

Grand Island
The Crisis Center
P.O. Box 1008
Grand Island, NE 68802
Hot Line: (308) 381-0555
Office: (308) 382-8250
Counties served: Hall, Howard,
    Merrick, Hamilton

Hastings
Spouse Abuse Sexual Assault Cri-
    sis Center
200 N. Burlington Ave. Suite 150
Hastings, NE 68901
Hot Line: (402) 463-4677
Office: (402) 463-5810
Counties served: Adams, Clay,
    Webster, Nuckolls

Kearney
The S.A.F.E. Center
3720 Avenue A, Suite C
Kearney, NE 68847
Hot Line / Office: (308) 237-2599
Counties served: Buffalo, Phelps,
    Harlan, Kearney, Franklin

Lexington
Dawson County Parent / Child
    Center
P.O. Box 722
Lexington, NE 68850
Hot Line: (308) 324-3040
Office: (308) 324-2336
Counties served: Dawson, Gosper

Lincoln
Friendship Home
P.O. Box 30268
Lincoln, NE 68503
Hot Line: (402) 475-7273
Office: (402) 474-4709
County served: Lancaster

Rape / Spouse Abuse Crisis Center
2545 N St.
Lincoln, NE 68510
Hot Line: (402) 475-RAPE
Office: (402) 476-2110

Macy
Macy Task Force on Domestic
 Violence
P.O. Box 307
Macy, NE 68039
Hot Line / Office: (402) 837-5302
Serves the Omaha Indian
 Reservation

McCook
Domestic Abuse / Sexual Assault
 Services
P.O. Box 714
McCook, NE 69001
Hot Line: (308) 345-1612
Office: (308) 345-5534
Counties served: Furnas, Hayes,
 Frontier, Hitchcock, Red
 Willow

Norfolk
Bright Horizons
P.O. Box 1711
Norfolk, NE 69701
Hot Line / Office; (402) 379-3798
Counties served: Boyd, Holt,
 Knox, Pierce, Madison, Stanton,
 Cuming, Antelope

North Platte
Rape / Domestic Abuse Program
P.O. Box 393
North Platte, NE 69101
Hot Line: (308) 532-0624
Office: (308) 534-3495
Counties served: Lincoln, Mc-
 Pherson, Logan, Hooker,
 Thomas

Ogallala
Sandhills Crisis Intervention
 Program
P.O. Box 22
Ogallala, NE 69153
Hot Line: (308) 284-8477
Office: (308) 284-6055
Counties served: Keith, Arthur,
 Grant, Deuel, Garden, Perkins

Omaha
USCC–The Shelter
P.O. Box 4346
Omaha, NE 68104
Hot Line / Office: (402) 558-5700
County served: Douglas

Women Against Violence
YWCA
222 S. 29th St.
Omaha, NE 68131
Hot Line: (402) 345-RAPE
Office: (402) 345-6555
County served: Douglas

Scottsbluff
Scottsbluff County Domestic Vio-
 lence, Inc.
P.O. Box 434
Scottsbluff, NE 69361
Hot Line: (308) 436-4357
Office: (308) 632-3683
Counties servied: Scotts Bluff, Box
 Butte, Sioux, Banner, Morrill,
 Kimball, Cheyenne

Valentine
North Central Quad County Task
Force Against Domestic Vio-
lence
421 E. 3rd St.
Valentine, NE 69201
Hot Line / Office: (402) 376-2045
Counties served: Cherry, Keya
Paha, Brown, Rock

Wayne
Haven House Family Service
Center
P.O. Box 44
Wayne, NE 68787
Hot Line / Office: (402) 375-4633
Counties served: Cedar, Dixon,
Wayne, Dakota, Thurston

NEVADA

Las Vegas
Community Action Against Rape
749 Veterans Memorial Dr.,
Room 150
Las Vegas, NV 89101
Hot Line: (702) 366-1640
Office: (702) 385-2153
Fax: (702) 385-7659

Reno
Suicide Prevention and Crisis Call
Center
P.O. Box 8016
Reno, NV 89507
Hot Line: (702) 323-6111
Hot Line: (800) 992-5757
Office: (702) 323-4533

NEW HAMPSHIRE

Manchester
Women's Crisis Line for Rape
Victims and Battered Women—
YWCA
72 Concord St.
Manchester, NH 03101
Hot Line / Office: (603) 668-2299

Nashua
Rape and Assault Support Services
10 Prospect St., P.O. Box 217
Nashua, NH 03061
Hot Line / Office: (603) 833-3044

NEW JERSEY

Belvidere
Rape Crisis Center
P.O. Box 423
Belvidere, NJ 07823
Hot Line / Office (908) 475-8408
County served: Warren

Cape May Court House
Coalition Against Rape and Abuse
P.O. Box 744
Cape May Court House, NJ 08210
(609) 522-6489
County served: Cape May

Collingswood
Women Against Rape (WAR)
P.O. Box 346
Collingswood, NJ 08108
Hot Line / Office: (609) 858-7800
Counties served: Burlington, Cam-
den, Gloucester

Flemington
Women's Crisis Services
Rape Care Program
47 East Main St.
Flemington, NJ 08822
Hot Line / Office: (908) 788-4044
County served: Hunterdon

Hackensack
Rape Crisis Center
285 Passaic St.
Hackensack, NJ 08108
Hot Line / Office: (201) 487-2227
County served: Bergen

Hazlet
Women's Center of Monmouth
County
Rape Care Program
1 Bethany Rd., Bldg. 3, Unit 42
Hazlet, NJ 07730
Hot Line / Office: (908) 264-RAPE
County served: Monmouth

Jersey City
Christ Hospital Mental Health
Center
Sexual Assault Service
176 Palisade Ave.
Jersey City, NJ 07306
Hot Line / Office: (201) 795-8375
County served: Hudson

Metuchen
Roosevelt Hospital
Rape Crisis Center
P.O. Box 151
Metuchen, NJ 08840
Hot Line / Office: (908) 321-6800
County served: Middlesex

Millville
Cumberland County Guidance
Center
Rape Care Program
P.O. Box 808, Carmel Rd. RD 1
Millville, NJ 08332
Hot Line / Office: (609) 455-5555
County served: Cumberland

Morristown
Morristown Memorial Hospital
Rape Care Program
100 Madison Ave., Box 6
Morristown, NJ 07960
Hot Line / Office: (201) 971-5648
County served: Morris

Newark
Sexual Assault Rape Analysis Unit
(SARA)
1 Lincoln Ave.
Newark, NJ 07104
Hot Line: (201) 733-RAPE
Office: (201) 268-8478

United Hospitals Medical Center
15 South 9th St.
Newark, NJ 07107
Hot Line / Office: (201) 268-8499

Newton
Newton Memorial Hospital
Sexual Assault Abuse
175 High St.
Newton, NJ 07860
Hot Line / Office: (201) 875-1211
County served: Sussex

Northfield
Atlantic County Women's Center
Rape Care Program
P.O. Box 311
Northfield, NJ 08225
Hot Line / Office: (609) 646-6767

Paterson
Passaic County Women's Services
Rape Care Program
P.O. Box 244
Paterson, NJ 07513
Hot Line / Office: (201) 881-1450
County served: Passaic

Salem
Salem County Women's Services
Rape Care Program
P.O. Box 125
Salem, NJ 08079
Hot Line / Office: (609) 935-6655
County served: Salem

Somerville
Rape Crisis Services of Somerset
95 Veterans Memorial Dr. East
Somerville, NJ 08876
Hot Line / Office: (908) 526-7444
County served: Somerset

Trenton
YWCA Rape Crisis Program
140 E. Hanover St.
Trenton, NJ 08608
Hot Line / Office: (609) 989-9332
County served: Mercer

Westfield
Rape Crisis Center
300 North Avenue East
Westfield, NJ 07090
Hot Line / Office: (908) 233-7273
County served: Union

NEW MEXICO

Alamogordo
HELPline Rape Crisis Team
Otero County Mental Health
  Association
1408 Eighth St.
Alamogordo, NM 88310
Hot Line / Office: (505) 437-8680

Hobbs
Crisis Line
Lea County Crisis Center, Inc.
920 W. Broadway
Hobbs, NM 88240
Hot Line / Office: (505) 393-6633

Portales
Roosevelt County Rape Crisis
  Advocacy
Mental Health Resources, Inc.
300 E. First St.
Portales, NM 88130
Hot Line: (505) 432-2159
Office: (505) 259-1221

Roswell
Counseling Associates, Inc.
108 West Bland St.
P.O. Box 1978
Roswell, NM 88202
Hot Line: (505) 623-1480
Office: (505) 622-3325

Santa Fe
Santa Fe Rape Crisis Center, Inc.
P.O. Box 2822
Santa Fe, NM 87504
Hot Line / Office: (505) 982-4667

Taos
Community Against Rape, Inc.
Box 3170
Taos, NM 87504
Hot Line / Office: (505) 758-2910

NEW YORK

Binghamton
Rape Crisis Center
56–58 Whitney Ave.
Binghamton, NY 13902
Hot Line / Office: (607) 722-4256

Buffalo
Volunteer Support
The Advocate Program
Crisis Services, Inc.
2969 Main St.
Buffalo, NY 11432-1385
Hot Line / Office: (716) 834-3131

New York City
Mount Sinai Medical Center
Rape Intervention Program
5th Ave. and 101st St.
New York, NY 10029
Hot Line / Office: (212) 241-5461

Rape Crisis Program
Department of Community
    Medicine
St. Vincent's Hospital
153 W. Eleventh St.
New York, NY 10011
Hot Line / Office: (212) 790-8068
    (day)
Hot Line / Office: (212) 604-8000
    (nights and weekends)

Oneonta
Oneonta Rape Crisis Network
c/o Opportunities for Otsego
3 W. Broadway
Oneonta, NY 13820
Hot Line: (607) 432-4855
Office: (607) 433-8320

Plattsburgh
Rape Crisis Program / Plattsburgh
    Community Crisis Center
29 Protection Ave.
Plattsburgh, NY 12901
Hot Line / Office: (518) 561-2330

Rochester
Rape Crisis Service of Planned
    Parenthood of Rochester and
    the Genesee Valley
114 University Ave.
Rochester, NY 14605
Hot Line / Office: (716) 546-2777
    (Monroe County)
Hot Line / Office: (800) 527-1757
    (Genesee, Orleans, Livingston
    Counties)

Schenectady
Rape Crisis Service of Schenectady, Inc.
c/o Planned Parenthood
414 Union St.
Schenectady, NY 12305
Hot Line / Office: (518) 346-2266

Syracuse
Rape Crisis Service of Syracuse,
Inc.
432 W. Onondaga St.
Syracuse, NY 13202-3288
Hot Line / Office: (315) 422-RAPE

NORTH CAROLINA

Asheville
Rape Crisis Center of Asheville
P.O. Box 7453
Asheville, NC 28807
Hot Line / Office: (704) 255-7576

Burlington
Rape Crisis Alliance of Alamance
County
Box 2573
Burlington, NC 27215
Hot Line: (910) 277-6220
Office: (910) 228-0813

Chapel Hill
Orange County Rape Crisis Center
406 W. Rosemary St.,
P.O. Box 871
Chapel Hill, NC 27514-0871
Hot Line: (916) 967-RAPE
Office: (916) 968-4647

Charlotte
Victim Assistance
720 East 4th St., Suite 204
Charlotte, NC 28202
Hot Line / Office: (704) 375-9900

Greenville
Rape Victim Companion Program
REAL Crisis Prevention, Inc.
600 E. Eleventh St.
Greenville, NC 27858
Hot Line / Office: (919) 758-0455

Salisbury
The Rape, Child and Family
Abuse Crises
Council of Salisbury–Rowan, Inc.
127 W. Council St.
Salisbury, NC 28144
Hot Line: (704) 636-9222
Office: (704) 636-4718

Statesville
Rape and Abuse Prevention
Group of Statesville / Iredell
County, Inc.
906 Fifth St.
Statesville, NC 28677
Hot Line / Office: (704) 872-7638

NORTH DAKOTA

Fargo
Rape and Abuse Crisis Center of
Fargo-Moorhead
317 North 8th St.
P.O. Box 2984
Fargo, ND 58108
Hot Line: (701) 293-7273
Hot Line: (800) 344-7273
Fax: (701) 293-9424

Grand Forks
Grand Forks Rape Crisis Center
111 South 4th St.
Grand Forks, ND 58201
Hot Line / Office: (701) 746-8900

OHIO

Akron
Akron Rape Crisis Center
146 S. High St.
Akron, OH 44308
Hot Line: (216) 434-RAPE
Office: (216) 253-6131

Canton
Rape Crisis Center
American Red Cross
618 Second St. NW
Canton, OH 44703
Hot Line / Office: (216) 452-1111

Cleveland
Rape Crisis Center
3101 Euclid Ave. #604
Cleveland, OH 44115
Hot Line / Office: (216) 391-3914

Columbus
Rape Crisis Center / Women
    Against Rape
P.O. Box 02084
Columbus, OH 43202
Hot Line / Office: (614) 221-4447

Toledo
Toledo United Against Rape
P.O. Box 4372
Toledo, OH 43609
Hot Line / Office: (419) 241-3235

Warren
Contact
1569 Woodland Ave. NE #10
Warren, OH 44483-5346
Hot Line: (216) 393-1565
Office: (216) 374-4060
TDD: (216) 393-1566
TDD: (216) 545-4372

OKLAHOMA

Enid
Rape Crisis Center
525 S. Quincy, P.O. Box 3165
Enid, OK 73701
Hot Line / Office: (405) 234-7644

Norman
Norman Shelter Crisis Center
P.O. Box 5089
Norman, OK 73701
Hot Line: (405) 360-0590
Office: (405) 364-9424

OREGON

Corvallis
Center Against Rape and Domes-
    tic Violence
216 S.W. Madison, P.O. Box 914
Corvallis, OR 97339
Hot Line: (503) 754-0110
Hot Line: (800) 927-0197
Office: (503) 758-0219

Oregon City
Victim Assistance Division
707 Main St., Suite 210
Oregon City, OR 97045
Hot Line / Office: (503) 655-8616

PENNSYLVANIA

Allentown
Rape Crisis Council of Lehigh
    Valley, Inc.
509 North 7th St.
Allentown, PA 18102
Hot Line / Office: (215) 437-6610

Altoona
Sexual Assault Volunteer Effort
Mental Health Center
Altoona Hospital
Howard Ave. and Seventh St.
Altoona, PA 16601
Hot Line / Office: (814) 946-2141

Butler
Center on Rape and Assault
    (CORA)
222 W. Cunningham St.
Butler, PA 16001
Hot Line / Office: (412) 282-RAPE
Fax: (412) 282-6990

Irene Stacy Community Mental
    Health Center
112 Hillvue Dr.
Butler, PA 16001
Hot Line / Office: (412) 287-0791

Doylestown
Doylestown Network of Victim
    Assistance
30 W. Oakland Ave.
Doylestown, PA 18901-4209
Hot Line: (215) 752-3596
Office: (215) 384-5664
Fax: (215) 340-9968
TDD: (215) 348-9263

Du Bois
Crisis Unit
Clearfield/Jefferson Community
    Mental Health Center
100 Caldwell Dr.
Du Bois, PA 15801
Hot Line: (814) 371-1105
Office: (814) 271-1100

East Stroudsburg
Women's Resources
400 Main St.
East Stroudsburg, PA 18360
Hot Line / Office: (717) 421-4200
Hot Line / Office: (717) 421-4000
    (night)

Harrisburg
Harrisburg Area Rape Crisis
    Center
215 Market St.
Harrisburg, PA 17101
Hot Line / Office: (717) 238-RAPE

Hazelton
Victims' Resource Center
107 Madison Ave.
West Hazelton, PA 18201
Hot Line / Office: (717) 454-7200

Lancaster
Lancaster Rape Aid and
    Prevention
110 N. Lime St.
Lancaster, PA 17602
Hot Line: (717) 392-RAPE
Office: (717) 393-1735

Meadville
Crisis Line
751 Liberty St.
Meadville, PA 16355
Hot Line / Office: (814) 724-2732

Media
Delaware County Women Against
Rape, Inc.
P.O. Box 211
Media, PA 19063
Hot Line / Office: (215) 566-4342

Norristown
Rape Crisis Center
P.O. Box 1179
Norristown, PA 19404
Hot Line / Office: (215) 277-5200

Philadelphia
Women Organized Against Rape
7233 Locust St.
Philadelphia, PA 19107
Hot Line / Office: (215) 985-3315

Pittsburgh
Action Against Rape
81 S. 19th St.
Pittsburgh, PA 15203
Hot Line / Office: (412) 413-5665

State College
Women's Resource Center / Rape
Abuse Services
140 West Nittany Ave.
State College, PA 16801-4881
Hot Line: (814) 234-5050
Office: (814) 234-5222

Tunkhannock
Victim's Resource Center
86 East Tioga St.
Tunkhannock, PA 18657
Hot Line / Office: (717) 836-5544

West Chester
Rape Crisis Council of Chester
County
Box 738
West Chester, PA 19381
Hot Line / Office: (215) 692-RAPE

Wilkes-Barre
Luzerne County Women Orga-
nized Against Rape (WOAR)
68 S. Franklin St.
Wilkes-Barre, PA 18701
Hot Line: (717) 823-0765
Office: (717) 823-0766

RHODE ISLAND

Providence
Rhode Island Rape Crisis Center
300 Richmond St., Suite 201
Providence, RI 02903
Hot Line / Office: (401) 421-4100

Women's Center of Rhode Island
16 Trenton St.
Providence, RI 02906
Hot Line / Office: (401) 861-2760

SOUTH CAROLINA

Florence
Pee Dee Coalition Against Domes-
tic and Sexual Assault
145 N. Irby St.
Florence, S.C. 29503
Hot Line / Office: (803) 669-4600

Greenville
Rape Crisis Council
104 Chapman St.
Greenville, SC 29605
Hot Line: (803) 467-3633
Office: (803) 467-3278

SOUTH DAKOTA

Aberdeen
Resource Center for Women
P.O. Box 41
Aberdeen, SD 57402-0041
Hot Line / Office: (605) 226-1212

TENNESSEE

Knoxville
Sexual Assault Crisis Center
P.O. Box 11523
Knoxville, TN 37939-1523
Hot Line: (615) 522-7273
Office: (615) 522-9040

Memphis
Comprehensive Rape Crisis
  Program
260 Poplar St., Suite 300
Memphis, TN 38122
Hot Line / Office: (901) 528-2161

TEXAS

Abilene
Abilene Rape Crisis Center
P.O. Box 122
Abilene, TX 79604
Hot Line / Office: (915) 677-7895

Amarillo
Rape Crisis and Sexual Abuse
  Service
900 South Lincoln
Amarillo, TX 79101
Hot Line: (806) 373-8022
Office: (806) 372-3202

Beaumont
Rape Crisis Center of Southeast
  Texas
P.O. Box 5011
Beaumont, TX 77706
Hot Line: (409) 835-3355
Office: (409) 832-6530

Killeen
Families-in-Crisis Center
P.O. Box 25
Killeen, TX 76540
Hot Line: 800-373-2774
Office: (817) 634-1184

Lubbock
Lubbock Rape Crisis Center
P.O. Box 2000
Lubbock, TX 79457
Hot Line: (806) 763-RAPE
Office: (806) 763-3232

Round Rock
Rape Crisis Center
211 Commerce Blvd., Suite 103
Round Rock, TX 78664-2164
Hot Line: (800) 460-SAFE
Office: (512) 255-1212

San Antonio
Rape Crisis Line
P.O. Box 27802
San Antonio, TX 78227
Hot Line: (210) 349-RAPE
Office: (210) 521-7273

Tyler
Rape Crisis Center
1314 South Fleishel
Tyler, TX 75701
Hot Line: (903) 595-5591
Office: (903) 595-3199

UTAH

Farmington
Intermountain Sexual Abuse Center (ISAC)
115 South 200 East
Farmington, UT 84025
Hot Line: (800) 303-9805
Office: (801) 451-6901

Salt Lake City
Intermountain Sexual Abuse Center (ISAC)
1800 Southwest Temple, Suite 421
P.O. Box 3624
Salt Lake City, UT 84110-3624
Hot Line / Office: (801) 486-9805

Ogden
Rape Crisis Center
2261 Adams Ave.
Ogden, UT 84401
Hot Line: (801) 392-7273

VERMONT

Burlington
Women's Rape Crisis Center
P.O. Box 92
Burlington, VT 05402
Hot Line: (802) 863-1236
Office: (802) 864-0555
TDD Available

Rutland
Rutland County Rape Crisis Team
Box 313
Rutland, VT 05401
Hot Line: (802) 775-3232
Office: (802) 775-6788

VIRGINIA

Alexandria
Fairfax Victim Assistance Network
8119 Holland Rd.
Alexandria, VA 22306
Hot Line: (703) 360-7273
Office: (703) 360-6910
TDD: (703) 799-8253

Sexual Assault Response and Awareness
110 North Royal St., Room 201
Alexandria, VA 22314
Hot Line: (703) 683-7273
Office: (703) 838-5030

Arlington
Arlington County Victims of Violence Program
1725 North George Mason Dr.
Arlington, VA 22205
Hot Line: (703) 358-4848
Office: (703) 358-5150

Bristol
Bristol Crisis Center
P.O. Box 642
Bristol, VA 24203
Hot Line: (703) 466-2312 or (703) 628-7731
Office: (703) 466-2218

Charlottesville
Charlottesville Rape Crisis Group
214 Rugby Rd., P.O. Box 6705
Charlottesville, VA 22906
Hot Line: (804) 977-RAPE

Danville
D.O.V.E.S. Rape Crisis Service
P.O. Box 2381
Danville, VA 24541
Hot Line: (804) 791-1400
Office: (804) 799-3683

Fredericksburg
Rappahannock Council Against
  Sexual Assault
P.O. Box 1276
Fredericksburg, VA 22402
Hot Line / Office: (703) 371-1666

Harrisonburg
Citizens Against Sexual Assault
P.O. Box 1473
Harrisonburg, VA 22801
Hot Line / Office: (703) 434-2272

Hopewell
Sexual Assault Outreach Program
The Women's Center—John Ran-
  dolph Hospital
411 W. Randolph Rd.
Hopewell, VA 23860
Hot Line: (804) 541-7791
Office: (804) 541-7795

Lexington
Rockbridge Area Coalition
  Against Sexual Assault
P.O. Box 414
Lexington, VA 24450
Hot Line / Office: (703) 463-7273

Lynchburg
Rape Crisis Companion Program
  Services
Crisis Line of Central Virginia,
  Inc.
P.O. Box 3074
Lynchburg, VA 24503
Hot Line: (804) 947-7273
Office: (804) 947-7422

Martinsville
Citizens Against Family Violence,
  Inc.
P.O. Box 210
Martinsville, VA 24114
Hot Line / Office: (703) 632-8701

Newport News
Contact Peninsula
Sexual Assault Services Program
P.O. Box 1006
Newport News, VA 23601
Hot Line: (804) 245-0041
Office: (804) 244-0594

Norfolk
Response
253 W. Freemason St.
Norfolk, VA 23510
Hot Line: (804) 622-4300
Office: (804) 623-2115
TDD: (804) 623-2115

Radford
Women's Resource Center of the
  New River Valley
P.O. Box 306
Radford, VA 24141
Hot Line: (703) 639-1123
Office: (703) 639-9592

Richmond
YWCA
6 North 5th St.
Richmond, VA 23219
Office: (804) 643-6761
Richmond: (804) 643-0888
Chesterfield: (804) 796-3066

Roanoke
Sexual Assault Response and
  Awareness
Blue Ridge Community Services
701-B Brandon Ave. S.W.
Roanoke, VA 24015
Hot Line: (703) 345-7273
Office: (703) 981-9352

Staunton
Blue Ridge Sexual Assault Center
P.O. Box 2415
Staunton, VA 24402
Hot Line / Office: (703) 885-7273

Tazewell
Victims of Sexual Assault
P.O. Box 487
Tazewell, VA 24651
Hot Line: (800) 752-2271
Office: (703) 988-5583

Williamsburg
Avalon: A Center for Women and
  Children
P.O. Box 1079
Williamsburg, VA 23187
Hot Line: (804) 258-5051
Office: (804) 258-5022

Winchester
Sexual Assault Support and Pre-
  vention Program
P.O. Box 14
Winchester, VA 22604
Hot Line / Office: (703) 667-6466

Woodbridge
ACTS Health Line
4331 Ridgewood Center Dr.
Woodbridge, VA 22193
Hot Line: (703) 368-4141
Office: (703) 680-7799

Wytheville
Family Resource Center, Inc.
Sexual Assault Program
P.O. Box 612
Wytheville, VA 24382
Hot Line: (703) 228-8431
Office: (703) 228-7141

WASHINGTON

Bellingham
Whatcom County Rape Relief
1407 Commercial St.
Bellingham, WA 98225
Hot Line: (206) 384-1485
Hot Line: (206) 671-5714

Bremerton
Rape Response
920 Park Ave., P.O. Box 1327
Bremerton, WA 98310
Hot Line / Office: (206) 479-1788

Olympia
Safe Place
P.O. Box 1605
Olympia, WA 98507
Hot Line / Office: (206) 754-6300

Renton
King County Rape Relief
305 S. Forty-third St.
Renton, WA 98055
Hot Line: (206) 226-RAPE
Office: (206) 226-5062

Seattle
Seattle Rape Relief
Counseling, Advocacy, &
  Education
1905 S. Jackson
Seattle, WA 98144
Hot Line: (206) 632-RAPE
Office: (206) 325-5531

Sexual Assault Center
Harborview Medical Center
325 Ninth Ave.
Seattle, WA 98104
Hot Line / Office: (206) 223-3047

Spokane
Lutheran Social Services
Symons Bldg., Suite 200
7 South Howard
Spokane, WA 99204
Hot Line: (509) 624-RAPE
Office: (509) 747-8224

Wenatchee
Wenatchee Rape Crisis and Do-
  mestic Violence Center
Chelan County Special Services
  Center
1203 South Mission St.
Wenatchee, WA 98801
Hot Line: (509) 663-7446
Hot Line: (800) 562-6025

Yakima
Rape Relief Program
Central Washington Comprehen-
  sive Mental Health Center
Great Western Bldg.
321 E. Yakima Ave.
Yakima, WA 98901
Hot Line / Office: (800) 572-8122

WEST VIRGINIA

Charleston
Mental Health Center
511 Morris St.
Charleston, WV 26505
Hot Line / Office: (304) 292-5100

YWCA
Resolve Family Abuse Program
1114 Quarrier St.
Charleston, WV 25301
Hot Line: 800-352-6513
Hot Line: (304) 340-3550
  (Charleston)
Hot Line: (304) 587-7243 (Clay)
Hot Line: (304) 369-4189
  (Madison)

Morgantown
Rape and Domestic Violence In-
  formation Center
P.O. Box 4228
Morgantown, WV 26505
Hot Line / Office: (304) 292-5100

Wheeling
Sexual Assault Help Center
P.O. Box 6764
Wheeling, WV 26003
Hot Line: (304) 234-8519
Office: (304) 234-1783

WISCONSIN

Green Bay

Green Bay Rape Crisis Center,
Ltd.
131 S. Madison
Green Bay, WI 54301
Hot Line / Office: (414) 436-8899

Madison

Dane County Project on Rape
312 E. Wilson St.
Madison, WI 53703
Hot Line / Office: (608) 251-RAPE
(7:00 p.m.–7:00 a.m.)

Rape Crisis Center, Inc.
128 East Olin Ave.
Madison, WI 53713
Hot Line: (608) 251-7273
Office: (608) 251-5126

Oshkosh

Winnebago County Rape Crisis
Center
201 Ceape Ave.
Oshkosh, WI 54901
Hot Line / Office: (414) 426-1460
(Oshkosh)
Hot Line / Office: (414) 722-8150
(Neenah, Menasha)

WYOMING

Casper

Self Help Center Inc.
341 East E St., Suite 135-A
Casper, WY 82601
Hot Line / Office: (307) 235-2814

Cheyenne

Safehouse / Sexual Assault and
Rape Crisis
P.O. Box 1885
Cheyenne, WY 82003-1885
Hot Line: (307) 637-7233
Office: (307) 634-8655

Jackson

Teton County Task Force
Family Violence and Sexual
Assault
P.O. Box 1328
Jackson, WY 83001
Hot Line: (307) 733-7466
Office: (307) 733-3711

Here are some tips to help you be as safe as possible at college. Before you arrive on campus, request information about security and the school's standard procedures when a theft or an assault is committed.

1. Go places with other people.
2. Use escort services whenever possible. Most college campuses have walking and van escort services that will pick you up wherever you are and take you wherever you need to go.
3. If you have to walk alone, always take the best-lit, most populated routes, even if they're out of the way; and know where the Blue Light emergency phones are, so that you can use them in an emergency.
4. Always lock your dorm room door and windows.
5. Don't prop open entrance doors. Everybody does it, but it also makes everyone more vulnerable.
6. Know what kind of security the university offers. Is it a security force or campus police? Police have the power to arrest; security-service personnel do not. How many people are on duty? What services do they provide?

7. Ask about crime statistics. The university is required to tell you; it's the law.
8. Find out about the women's center on campus; it may have important information on safety issues.

Of course, it's up to you to make your own decisions about drugs and alcohol; but while under the influence, you greatly increase your risk of doing something stupid. Here are some precautions.

1. Go to parties with a group of people. Look out for one another. If you want to get together with a guy, make sure a friend knows where you are. Take into account how much the guy has had to drink and how well he can hold his alcohol.
2. Have friends you can trust. If you are drunk and require help or want to go home, you need someone dependable to assist you.
3. If you are going to experiment with drugs, make sure you do so in familiar surroundings with people you know well and trust.

Overall, the most important way to ensure your safety is to think about what you are doing. Ask yourself, "Am I putting myself at risk by doing this?" If the answer is yes, make a decision that is in your own best interest.

If you are concerned about your daughter's physical safety, whether it is going out for the evening or going away to college, you are not alone. Many parents worry about their daughters. Unfortunately, some parents are dealing with a child who either is in a dangerous relationship or has been raped. The pain in their faces makes me realize how difficult it must have been for my own parents to watch me as a teenager, because I refused their help. What can I tell you to do? Educate yourself about the problem, and realize that no matter how protective and caring you are or try to be, you can't shield your daughter from everything. If she is in a dangerous relationship, she will have to get out of it on her own. She will not change her situation unless she wants to. She will depend on your support and love (even though she may not recognize it at the time), but you can't force her to get help or make decisions that you think are best for her. The most constructive thing you can do is tell her you are there for her whenever she wants to talk, and tell her over and over again that everyone (including you) makes bad decisions or mistakes sometimes. If you keep telling her this, she will know she can come to you for help without being judged.